The challenge of the faith and of our present KAIROS
is addressed to all who bear the name Christian. . . .
We see the present crisis,
or KAIROS,
as indeed a divine visitation.

—*Kairos Document, Conclusion*

THE KAIROS COVENANT

Standing with South African Christians

EDITED BY WILLIS H. LOGAN

Friendship Press • New York

Published in the United States by Meyer-Stone Books,
a division of Meyer, Stone, and Company, Inc.,
714 South Humphrey, Oak Park, IL 60304
and

Friendship Press, 475 Riverside Drive, New York, NY 10115

Kairos Document, second edition,
copyright © 1986 by the ICT on behalf of the Kairos theologians

Cover design: Terry Dugan Design

Manufactured in the United States of America
92 91 90 89 88   5 4 3 2 1

Library of Congress Cataloging in Publication Data

The Kairos covenant
    Includes bibliographical references.
    1. Theology, Doctrinal — South Africa — History — 20th
century. 2. Kairos Theologians (Group) 3. Race
relations — Religious aspects — Christianity. I. Logan,
Willis H., 1945-
BT30.S5K33   1988   261.7'0968   87-62870
ISBN 0-940989-29-8 (Meyer-Stone Books)
ISBN 0-377-00189-9 (Friendship Press)

Contents

Preface

The Kairos Document is a *prophetic* theological statement that presents a direct challenge to all Christians inside and outside South Africa. The document speaks to the nature of the injustice that is apartheid, and it also speaks to the nature of the sin committed by permitting such an evil system of human exploitation to exist. It is a profound appeal for reflection and action.

As part of our effort to respond to the challenge presented by the Kairos Document, the Africa Committee of the National Council of Churches organized a convocation on the Kairos Document in November 1986 in Chicago. The meeting was convened in order to provide an opportunity for Christians in the United States to come together and reflect on the Kairos Document and formulate appropriate responses to the situation in South Africa.

The convocation was organized around the major sections of the Kairos Document: State Theology, Church Theology, Prophetic Theology. This volume contains all the formal presentations and most of the responses to those presentations. In addition, the Kairos Covenant and the Sing Sing statement have been included as examples of responses of U.S. Christians to the Kairos Document. The Kairos Covenant was the collective response of the participants in the convocation; the Sing Sing statement was produced through a process of study and reflection on the Kairos Document conducted by inmates at Sing Sing Correctional Facility in New York and was used as one of the preparatory documents for the convocation.

The final section of the volume is a study guide for the Kairos Document.

We gratefully acknowledge the assistance of Burgess Carr, Audrey Glover, and John Eagleson, as well as that of the Trinity Grants Program in the preparation of this volume.

The Kairos Document is a treasure, both hidden and revealed. What you have in this book is a key, a resource to unlock the document's power. It is our hope that by studying the document itself, by digesting the reflections of others, by delving into Scripture, and by wrestling with the issues out of your own experience, you will come to a "kairos covenant," a covenant that empowers you to rise and stand with South African Christians.

WILLIS H. LOGAN
Director, Africa Committee
Division of Overseas Ministries
National Council of Churches

Part One
THE KAIROS DOCUMENT

The Kairos Document

PREFACE

The Kairos Document is a Christian, biblical, and theological comment on the political crisis in South Africa today. It is an attempt by concerned Christians in South Africa to reflect on the situation of death in our country. It is a critique of the current theological models that determine the type of activities the church engages in to try to resolve the problems of the country. It is an attempt to develop, out of this perplexing situation, an alternative biblical and theological model that will in turn lead to forms of activity that will make a real difference to the future of our country.

Of particular interest is *the way* the theological material was produced. In June 1985 as the crisis was intensifying in the country, as more and more people were killed, maimed, and imprisoned, as one black township after another revolted against the apartheid regime, as the people refused to be oppressed or to cooperate with oppressors, facing death by the day, and as the apartheid army moved into the townships to rule by the barrel of the gun, a number of theologians who were concerned about the situation expressed the need to reflect on this situation to determine what response by the church and by all Christians in South Africa would be most appropriate.

A first discussion group met at the beginning of July in the heart of Soweto. Participants spoke freely about the situation and the various responses of the church, church leaders, and Christians. A critique of these responses was made and the theology from which these responses flowed was also subjected to a critical analysis. Individual members of the group were assigned to put together material on specific themes which were raised during the discussion and to present the material to the next session of the group.

At the second meeting the material itself was subjected to a critique, and various people were commissioned to do more investigations on specific problematic areas. The latest findings with the rest of the material were collated and presented to the third meeting, where more than thirty people, consisting of theologians, ordinary Christians (lay theologians), and some church leaders came together.

After a very extensive discussion some adjustments and additions were made especially in regard to the section entitled "Challenge to Action." The group then appointed a committee to subject the document to further critique by various other Christian groupings throughout the country. Everybody was told that "this was a people's document which you can also own even by demolishing it if your position can stand the test of biblical faith and Christian experience in South Africa." They were told that this was an open-ended document which will never be said to be final.

The "Working Committee," as it was called, was inundated with comments, suggestions, and enthusiastic appreciation from various groups and individuals in the country. By the 13th September 1985, when the document was submitted for publication, there were still comments and recommendations flowing in. The first publication therefore must be taken as a beginning, a basis for further discussion by all Christians in the country. Further editions will be published later.

September 25, 1985
Johannesburg

PREFACE
TO THE REVISED SECOND EDITION

It is exactly one year since the publication of the first edition of the Kairos Document. At that time, we said that "South Africa has been plunged into a crisis that is shaking the foundations and *there is every indication that the crisis has only just begun* and that *it will deepen and become even more threatening in the months to come.*" Today, one year later, the situation in South Africa is indeed far worse than before and the crisis far more serious.

A year ago we had a partial state of emergency; now we have a total, national state of emergency. Then one could, to a certain extent, report about what was happening in South Africa; now there is almost a total blackout of news. Then there were threats of sanctions; now it is a matter of what type of sanctions to apply against South Africa. There is more repression now than ever before, with thousands of people in detention, many missing, and some restricted or deported. While the Botha regime is going all out to demonstrate its power and its determination to maintain apartheid at all cost, the people have become more determined than ever to resist this regime even at the cost of their lives. This is indeed frightening. It is a *real kairos!*

The message of the Kairos Document has lost none of its relevance. If anything, it is more relevant today than it was a year ago. The Kairos theologians have therefore decided to publish a second edition of the document.

After extensive discussions among the Kairos theologians and with regional groups around the country, and after considering all the contributions from various groups, churches, and other persons here and abroad, and further, because of a desire to keep the document as simple as possible for easy reading by ordinary people, the editing of the document has been kept to a minimum. Amendments, elaborations, and additions have been made only where it was absolutely necessary for greater clarity. We have tried to maintain the quality of the first edition, its mood, sharpness, vigor, and simplicity, because this is what the signatories and others demanded. It had to be left as a prophetic word, a proclamation.

For this reason, no *debates* on the various themes raised by the first edition have been entered into. To meet this need the Kairos theologians are working on a book which will deal with the debates more scientifically. The publication of this book is scheduled for the middle of next year.

The only chapter of the original Kairos Document which has been almost completely rewritten is that on Prophetic Theology. It was generally felt that this chapter was not well developed in the first edition. Otherwise we have added explanatory notes to help clarify some points. Also, because of the thousands of people who wanted to have their *names* put to the document, it has not been possible to include a list of signatories in this edition. It would have made the edition too voluminous. We are nevertheless keeping a record of the list.

Responses to the first edition were overwhelming. The document has generated more discussions and debates than any previous theological document in South Africa. There has been overwhelming excitement about it in the black townships. It reinforced the people's faith and hope for a new and just society in South Africa. It came as an empowering instrument of faith committing them more than ever before to the struggle for justice and peace in South Africa. It was welcomed as a statement of what it means to be truly Christian in a violent apartheid society. For many, the Gospel became "Good News" for the first time in their lives.

The document also had a mission dimension. Many of those who had abandoned the church as an irrelevant institution that supports, justifies, and legitimizes this cruel apartheid system began to feel that if the church becomes the church as expounded by the Kairos Document then they would go back to church again. Even those who would consider themselves to be "non-Christians" in the conventional sense began to say that if this is Christianity they could become Christians.

There have also been responses from some of the churches in South Africa, from various Christian groups around the country, and from individual theologians and various other persons. And we have received volumes of responses from our sister churches around the world. All were very helpful in advancing the development of an authentic and relevant theology that addresses itself to the issues of the day. Like any other challenging material the document has also been viciously attacked, mostly by conservative church groups like the "Gospel Defence League" and "Christian Mission International." They actually called for the banning of the document. This came as no surprise to us as they are known for their support of the apartheid regime in South Africa and their attack on anyone who challenges this regime.

It might be interesting to study the relationship between the various individuals and groups who viciously attacked the document and those who welcomed it. For example, how does the theological stance relate to the class position or the social, economic, racial, and political interests of these groups of individuals? What is clear is that most of those who attacked the document failed to appreciate the *concerns* of those who participated in producing the document. They looked at the document from their own situation or context, which is completely different from that of the participants whose experience and ministry come from the townships. Most of the critics simply took the document out of its context and analyzed it in the realm of abstraction.

To appreciate the Kairos Document one needs to understand and internalize the concerns of those who produced it. Those Christians who live in the townships and who are experiencing the civil war that is tearing their lives apart understand immediately what the Kairos theologians are attempting to say; while those who do not have this experience find it difficult to understand the document.

Perhaps the most exciting and most important contribution of the Kairos Document has been its method, or way, of doing theology. Many Christians here and abroad are using the model or method of the Kairos Document to reflect on their own situation. They have begun to criticize the traditional, historical alignment of the church with Western ideology, institutions, and governments while those in the East are grappling with the question of how to live one's faith in socialist societies.

Against this background we publish today this second edition of the Kairos Document. It was developed in the same way as the first edition, except that thousands of people have been involved in the process, not only in terms of reflection and study but mostly in terms of involvement and action in the liberation struggle in South Africa. We hope that this edition will not be the end of the process of action and theological reflection on our situation. We hope that it will serve as a never-ending stimulus to keep the cycle of action-reflection-action moving forward.

September 1986

CHAPTER ONE

THE MOMENT OF TRUTH

The time has come. The moment of truth has arrived. South Africa has been plunged into a crisis that is shaking the foundations, and there is every indication that the crisis has only just begun and that it will deepen and become even more threatening in the months to come. It is the *kairos*,[1] or moment of truth, not only for apartheid but also for the church and all other faiths and religions.[2]

We as a group of theologians have been trying to understand the theological significance of this moment in our history. It is serious, very serious. For very many Christians in South Africa this is the *kairos*, the moment of grace and opportunity, the favorable time in which God issues a challenge to decisive action. It is a dangerous time because, if this opportunity is missed and allowed to pass by, the loss for the church, for the gospel, and for all the people of South Africa will be immeasurable. Jesus wept over Jerusalem. He wept over the tragedy of the destruction of the city and the massacre of the people that was imminent, "and all because you did not recognize your opportunity (*kairos*) when God offered it" (Luke 19:44).

A crisis is a judgment that brings out the best in some people and the worst in others. A crisis is a moment of truth that shows us up for what we really are. There will be no place to hide and no way of pretending to be what we are not in fact. At this moment in South Africa the church is about to be shown up for what it really is and no cover-up will be possible.

What the present crisis shows up, although many of us have known it all along, is that *the church is divided*. More and more people are now saying that there are in fact two churches in South Africa — a white church and a black church. Even within the same denomination there are in fact two churches. In the life and death conflict between different social forces that has come to a head in South Africa today, there are Christians (or at least people who profess to be Christians) on both sides of the conflict — and some who are trying to sit on the fence!

Does this prove that Christian faith has no real meaning or relevance for our times? Does it show that the Bible can be used for any purpose at all? Such problems would be critical enough for the church in any circumstances but when we also come to see that the conflict in South Africa is between the oppressor and the oppressed,[3] the crisis for the church as an institution becomes much more acute.[4] Both oppressor and oppressed claim loyalty to the same church. They are both baptized in the same baptism and participate together in the breaking of the same bread, the same body and blood of Christ. There we sit in the same church while outside Christian policemen and soldiers are beating up and killing Christian children or torturing Christian prisoners to death while yet other Christians stand by and weakly plead for peace.

The church is divided against itself[5] and its day of judgment has come.

The moment of truth has compelled us to analyze more carefully the different theologies in our churches and to speak out more clearly and boldly about the real significance of these theologies. We have been able to isolate three theologies and we have chosen to call them "State Theology," "Church Theology," and "Prophetic Theology."[6] In our thoroughgoing criticism of the first and second theologies we do not wish to mince our words. The situation is too critical for that.

CHAPTER TWO

CRITIQUE OF STATE THEOLOGY

The South African apartheid State has a theology of its own, and we have chosen to call it "State Theology." State Theology is simply the theological justification of the status quo with its racism, capitalism, and totalitarianism. It blesses injustice, canonizes the will of the powerful, and reduces the poor to passivity, obedience, and apathy.[7]

How does State Theology do this? It does it by misusing theological concepts and biblical texts for its own political purposes. In this document we would like to draw your attention to four key examples of how this is done in South Africa. The first would be the use of Romans 13:1-7 to give an absolute and "divine" authority to the State. The second would be the use of the idea of "Law and Order" to determine and control what the people may be permitted to regard as just and unjust. The third would be the use of the word "communist" to brand anyone who rejects State Theology. And finally there is the use that is made of the name of God.

2.1 Romans 13:1–7

The text reads as follows:

[1] You must all obey the governing authorities. Since all government comes from God, the civil authorities were appointed by God.

[2] And so anyone who resists authority is rebelling against God's decision, and such an act is bound to be punished.

[3] Good behavior is not afraid of magistrates; only criminals have anything to fear. If you want to live without being afraid of authority, you must live honestly and authority may even honor you.

[4] The State is there to serve God for your benefit. If you break the law, however, you may well have fear: the bearing of the sword has its significance. The authorities are there to serve God: they carry out God's revenge by punishing wrongdoers.

[5] You must obey, therefore, not only because you are afraid of being punished, but also for conscience' sake.

[6] This is also the reason why you must pay taxes, since all government officials are God's officers. They serve God by collecting taxes.
[7] Pay every government official what he has a right to ask — whether it be direct tax or indirect, fear or honor.

[Rom. 13:1–7][8]

The misuse of this famous text is not confined to the present government in South Africa. Throughout the history of Christianity totalitarian regimes have tried to legitimize an attitude of blind obedience and absolute servility towards the State by quoting this text. "As soon as Christians, out of loyalty to the gospel of Jesus, offer resistance to a State's totalitarian claim, the representatives of the State or their collaborationist theological advisers are accustomed to appeal to this saying of Paul, as if Christians are here commended to endorse and thus to abet all the crimes of a totalitarian State."[9]

But what then is the meaning of Romans 13:1–7 and why is the use made of it by State Theology unjustifiable from a biblical point of view?

State Theology assumes that in this text Paul is presenting us with the absolute and definitive Christian doctrine about the State, in other words an absolute and universal principle that is equally valid for all times and in all circumstances. The falseness of this assumption has been pointed out by numerous biblical scholars.[10]

What has been overlooked here is one of the most fundamental of all principles of biblical interpretation: every text must be interpreted *in its context*. To abstract a text from its context and to interpret it in the abstract is to distort the meaning of God's Word. Moreover the context here is not only the chapters and verses that precede and succeed this particular text nor is it even limited to the total context of the Bible. The context includes also the *circumstances* in which Paul's statement was made. Paul was writing to a particular Christian community in Rome, a community that had its own particular problems in relation to the State at that time and in those circumstances. That is part of the context of our text.

Many authors have drawn attention to the fact that in the rest of the Bible God does not demand obedience to oppressive rulers. Examples can be given ranging from Pharaoh to Pilate and through into Apostolic times. The Jews and later the Christians did not believe that their imperial overlords, the Egyptians, the Babylonians, the Greeks, or the Romans, had some kind of divine right to rule them and oppress them. These empires were the beasts described in the Book of Daniel and the Book of Revelation. God *allowed* them to rule for a while but he did not *approve* of what they did. It was not God's will. His will was the freedom and liberation of Israel. Romans 13:1–7 cannot be contradicting all of this.

But most revealing of all is the circumstances of the Roman Christians to whom Paul was writing. They were not revolutionaries. They were not trying to overthrow the State. They were not calling for a change of government. They were what has been called "antinomians" or "enthusiasts," and their belief was that Christians, and only Christians, were exonerated from obeying any State at all, any government or political authority at all, *because* Jesus alone was their Lord and King. This is of course heretical, and Paul is compelled to point out to these Christians that before the second coming of Christ there will always be some kind of State, some kind of secular government, and that Christians are not exonerated from subjection to some kind of political authority.

Paul is simply not addressing the issue of a just or unjust State or the need to change one government for another. He is simply establishing the fact that there will be some kind of secular authority and that Christians as such are not exonerated from subjection to secular laws and authorities. *"The State is there to serve God for your benefit,"* says Paul. That is the kind of State he is speaking of. That is the kind of State that must be obeyed. In this text Paul does not tell us what we should do when a State does *not* serve God and does *not* work for the benefit of all but has become unjust and oppressive. That is another question.

If we wish to search the Bible for guidance in a situation where the State that is supposed to be "the servant to God" betrays that calling and begins to serve Satan instead, then we can study chapter 13 of the Book of Revelation. Here the Roman State becomes the servant of the dragon (the devil) and takes on the appearance of a horrible beast. Its days are numbered because God will not permit his unfaithful servant to reign forever.

Consequently those who try to find answers to the very different questions and problems of our time in the text of Romans 13:1–7 are doing a great disservice to Paul. The use that State Theology makes of this text tells us more about the political options of those who construct this theology than it does about the meaning of God's Word in this text. As one biblical scholar puts it: "The primary concern is to justify the interests of the State and the text is pressed into its service without respect for the context and the intention of Paul."

2.2   Law and Order

The State makes use of the concept of law and order to maintain the status quo which it depicts as "normal." But this *law* is the unjust and discriminatory laws of apartheid, and this *order* is the organized and institutionalized disorder of oppression. Anyone who wishes to change this law and this order is made to feel that they are lawless and disorderly. In other words they are made to feel guilty of sin.

It is indeed the duty of the State to maintain law and order, but it has no divine mandate to maintain any kind of law and order. Something does not become moral and just simply because the State has declared it to be a law, and the organization of a society is not a just and right order simply because it has been instituted by the State. We cannot accept any kind of law and any kind of order. The concern of Christians is that we should have in our country a just law and a right order.

In the present crisis and especially during the State of Emergency, State Theology has tried to re-establish the status quo of orderly discrimination, exploitation, and oppression by appealing to the consciences of its citizens in the name of law and order. It tries to make those who reject this law and this order feel that they are ungodly. The State here is not only usurping the right of the church to make judgments about what would be right and just in our circumstances; it is going even further than that and demanding of us, in the name of law and order, an obedience that must be reserved for God alone. The South African State recognizes no authority beyond itself and therefore it will not allow anyone to question what it has chosen to define as "law and order." However, there are millions of Christians in South Africa today who are saying with Peter: "We must obey God rather than man [human beings]" (Acts 5:29).

State Theology further believes that the government has the

God-given right to use *violence* to enforce its system of "law and order." It bases this on Romans 13:4: "The authorities are there to serve God: they carry out God's revenge by punishing wrongdoers." In this way *state security* becomes a more important concern than *justice*, and those who in the name of God work to change the unjust structures of society are branded as ungodly agitators and rebels. The State often admonishes church leaders to "preach the pure gospel" and not to "meddle in politics," while at the same time it indulges in its own political theology which claims God's approval for its use of violence in maintaining an unjust system of "law and order."

The State appeals to the consciences of Christians in the name of "law and order" to accept this use of violence as a God-given duty, in order to re-establish the status quo of oppression. In this way people are sacrificed for the sake of laws, rather than laws for the sake of people, as in the life of Jesus: "The sabbath was made for man [the human person]; not man [the human person] for the sabbath" (Mark 2:27). The State's efforts to preserve law and order, which should imply the protection of human life, means the very opposite for the majority of the people, namely the suppression and destruction of life.

2.3   The Threat of Communism

We all know how the South African State makes use of the label "communist." Anything that threatens the status quo is labelled "communist." Anyone who opposes the State and especially anyone who rejects its theology is simply dismissed as a "communist." No account is taken of what communism really means. No thought is given to why some people have indeed opted for communism or for some form of socialism. Even people who have not rejected capitalism are called "communists" when they reject State Theology. The State uses the label "communist" in an uncritical and unexamined way as its symbol of evil.

State Theology like every other theology needs to have its own concrete symbol of evil. It must be able to symbolize what it regards as godless behavior and what ideas must be regarded as atheistic. It must have its own version of hell. And so it has invented, or rather taken over, the myth of communism. All evil is communistic and all communist or socialist ideas are atheistic

and godless. Threats about hell-fire and eternal damnation are
replaced by threats and warnings about the horrors of a tyrannical,
totalitarian, atheistic, and terrorist communist regime — a kind of
hell-on-earth. This is a very convenient way of frightening some
people into accepting any kind of domination and exploitation by
a capitalist minority.

The South African State has its own heretical theology, and according to that theology millions of Christians in South Africa (not
to mention the rest of the world) are to be regarded as "atheists."
It is significant that in earlier times when Christians rejected the
gods of the Roman Empire they were branded as "atheists" — by
the State.

2.4   The God of the State

The State in its oppression of the people makes use again and
again of the name of God. Military chaplains use it to encourage the South African Defense Force, police chaplains use it to
strengthen policemen, and cabinet ministers use it in their propaganda speeches. But perhaps the most revealing of all is the
blasphemous use of God's holy name in the preamble to the new
apartheid constitution.

> In humble submission to Almighty God, who controls the
> destinies of nations and the history of peoples; who gathered
> our forebears together from many lands and gave them this
> their own; who has guided them from generation to genera-
> tion; who has wondrously delivered them from the dangers
> that beset them.

This god is an idol. It is as mischievous, sinister, and evil as any
of the idols that the prophets of Israel had to contend with. Here
we have a god who is historically on the side of the white settlers,
who dispossesses black people of their land and who gives the major
part of the land to his "chosen people."

It is the god of superior weapons who conquered those who
were armed with nothing but spears. It is the god of the casspirs
and hippos, the god of teargas, rubber bullets, sjamboks, prison
cells, and death sentences. Here is a god who exalts the proud
and humbles the poor — the very opposite of the God of the Bible
who "scatters the proud of heart, pulls down the mighty from

their thrones, and exalts the humble" (Luke 1:51–52). From a theological point of view the opposite of the God of the Bible is the devil, Satan. The god of the South African State is not merely an idol or false god; it is the devil disguised as Almighty God — the antichrist.

The oppressive South African regime will always be particularly abhorrent to Christians precisely because it makes use of Christianity to justify its evil ways. As Christians we simply cannot tolerate this blasphemous use of God's name and God's Word. State Theology is not only heretical, it is blasphemous. Christians who are trying to remain faithful to the God of the Bible are even more horrified when they see that there are churches, like the White Dutch Reformed churches and other groups of Christians, who actually subscribe to this heretical theology. State Theology needs its own prophets and it manages to find them from the ranks of those who profess to be ministers of God's Word in some of our churches. What is particularly tragic for a Christian is to see the number of people who are fooled and confused by these false prophets and their heretical theology.

South African State Theology can be compared with the Court Theology of Israel's Kings, and our false prophets can be compared with the Court Prophets of Israel, of whom it is said:

> They have misled my people by saying: Peace! when there is no peace. Instead of my people rebuilding the wall, these men come and slap on plaster. I mean to shatter the wall you slapped with plaster, to throw it down and lay its foundations bare. It will fall and you will perish under it; and so you will learn that I am Yahweh. (Ezek. 13:10, 14)

CHAPTER THREE

CRITIQUE OF CHURCH THEOLOGY

We have analyzed the statements that are made from time to time by the so-called English-speaking churches. We have looked at what church leaders tend to say in their speeches and press statements about the apartheid regime and the present crisis. What we found running through all these pronouncements is a series of interrelated theological assumptions. These we have chosen to call "Church Theology." We are well aware of the fact that this theology does *not* express the faith of the majority of Christians in South Africa today who form the greater part of most of our churches. Nevertheless the opinions expressed by church leaders are regarded in the media and generally in our society as the official opinions of the churches.[11] We have therefore chosen to call these opinions Church Theology. The crisis in which we find ourselves today compels us to question this theology, to question its assumptions, its implications, and its practicality.

In a limited, guarded, and cautious way this theology is critical of apartheid. Its criticism, however, is superficial and counterproductive because instead of engaging in an in-depth analysis of the signs of our times, it relies upon a few stock ideas derived from Christian tradition and then uncritically and repeatedly applies them to our situation. The stock ideas used by almost all these church leaders that we would like to examine here are: reconciliation (or peace), justice, and non-violence.

3.1 Reconciliation

There can be no doubt that our Christian faith commits us to work for *true* reconciliation and *genuine* peace. But as so many people, including Christians, have pointed out there can be no true reconciliation and no genuine peace *without justice*. Any form of peace or reconciliation that allows the sin of injustice and oppression to continue is a *false* peace and *counterfeit* reconciliation. This kind of "reconciliation" has nothing whatsoever to do with the Christian faith.

Church Theology is not always clear on this matter and many Christians have been led to believe that what we need in South

Africa is not justice but reconciliation and peace. The argument goes something like this: "We must be fair. We must listen to both sides of the story. If the two sides can only meet to talk and negotiate they will sort out their differences and misunderstandings, and the conflict will be resolved." On the face of it this may sound very Christian. But is it?

The fallacy here is that "reconciliation" has been made into an absolute principle that must be applied in all cases of conflict or dissension. But not all cases of conflict are the same. We can imagine a private quarrel between two people or two groups whose differences are based upon misunderstandings. In such cases it would be appropriate to talk and negotiate to sort out the misunderstandings and to reconcile the two sides. But there are other conflicts in which one side is right and the other wrong. There are conflicts where one side is a fully armed and violent oppressor while the other side is defenseless and oppressed. There are conflicts that can only be described as the struggle between justice and injustice, good and evil, God and the devil. To speak of reconciling these two is not only a mistaken application of the Christian idea of reconciliation, it is a total betrayal of all that Christian faith has ever meant. Nowhere in the Bible or in Christian tradition has it ever been suggested that we ought to try to reconcile good and evil, God and the devil. We are supposed to do away with evil, injustice, oppression, and sin — not come to terms with it. We are supposed to oppose, confront, and reject the devil and not try to sup with the devil.

In our situation in South Africa today it would be totally un-Christian to plead for reconciliation and peace before the present injustices have been removed. Any such plea plays into the hands of the oppressor by trying to persuade those of us who are oppressed to accept our oppression and to become reconciled to the intolerable crimes that are committed against us. That is not Christian reconciliation, it is sin. It is asking us to become accomplices in our own oppression, to become servants of the devil. No reconciliation is possible in South Africa *without justice,* without the total dismantling of apartheid.

What this means in practice is that no reconciliation, no forgiveness, and no negotiations are possible *without repentance.* The biblical teaching on reconciliation and forgiveness makes it quite clear that nobody can be forgiven and reconciled with God unless

he or she repents of their sins. Nor are *we* expected to forgive the
unrepentant sinner. When he or she repents we must be willing to
forgive seventy times seven times, but before that we are expected
to preach repentance to those who sin against us or against anyone. Reconciliation, forgiveness, and negotiations will become our
Christian duty in South Africa only when the apartheid regime
shows signs of genuine repentance.[12] The State of Emergency, the
continued military repression of the people in the townships, and
the jailing of all its opponents is clear proof of the total lack of
repentance on the part of the present regime.

There is nothing that we want more than true reconciliation
and genuine peace — the peace that God wants and not the peace
the world wants (John 14:27). The peace that God wants is based
upon truth, repentance, justice, and love. The peace that the
world offers us is a unity that compromises the truth, covers over
injustice and oppression, and is totally motivated by selfishness.
At this stage, like Jesus, we must expose this false peace, confront
our oppressors, and be prepared for the dissension that will follow.
As Christians we must say with Jesus: "Do you suppose that I am
here to bring peace on earth. No, I tell you, but rather dissension"
(Luke 12:51). There can be no real peace without justice and
repentance.

It would be quite wrong to try to preserve "peace" and "unity"
at all costs, even at the cost of truth and justice and, worse still,
at the cost of thousands of young lives. As disciples of Jesus we
should rather promote truth and justice and life at all costs, even at
the cost of creating conflict, disunity, and dissension along the way.
To be truly biblical our church leaders must adopt a theology that
millions of Christians have already adopted — a biblical theology of
direct confrontation with the forces of evil rather than a theology
of reconciliation with sin and the devil.

3.2   Justice

It would be quite wrong to give the impression that Church Theology in South Africa is not particularly concerned about the need
for justice. There have been some very strong and very sincere demands for justice. But the question we need to ask here, the very
serious theological question is: What kind of justice? An examina-
tion of church statements and pronouncements gives the distinct

impression that the justice that is envisaged is *the justice of re-form,* that is to say, a justice that is determined by the oppressor, by the white minority, and that is offered to the people as a kind of concession. It does not appear to be the more radical justice that comes from below and is determined by the people of South Africa.

One of our main reasons for drawing this conclusion is the simple fact that almost all church statements and appeals are made to the State or to the white community. The assumption seems to be that changes must come from whites or at least from people who are at the top of the pile. The general idea appears to be that one must simply appeal to the conscience and the goodwill of those who are responsible for injustice in our land and that once they have repented of their sins and after some consultation with others they will introduce the necessary reforms to the system. Why else would church leaders be having talks with P. W. Botha if this is not the vision of a just and peaceful solution to our problems?

At the heart of this approach is the reliance upon "individual conversions" in response to "moralizing demands" to change the structures of a society. It has not worked and it never will work. The present crisis with all its cruelty, brutality, and callousness is ample proof of the ineffectiveness of years and years of Christian "moralizing" about the need for love. The problem that we are dealing with here in South Africa is not merely a problem of personal guilt, it is a problem of structural injustice. People are suffering, people are being maimed and killed and tortured every day. We cannot just sit back and wait for the oppressor to see the light so that the oppressed can put out their hands and beg for the crumbs of some small reforms. That in itself would be degrading and oppressive.

There have been reforms and, no doubt, there will be further reforms in the near future. And it may well be that the church's appeal to the consciences of whites has contributed marginally to the introduction of some of these reforms. But can such reforms ever be regarded as real change, as the introduction of a true and lasting justice? Reforms that come from the top are never satisfactory. They seldom do more than make the oppression more effective and more acceptable. If the oppressor does ever introduce reforms that might lead to real change this will come about because of strong pressure from those who are oppressed. True justice, God's justice, demands a radical change of structures. This can only come from below, from the oppressed themselves. God will bring about change through the oppressed as he did through the oppressed Hebrew slaves in Egypt. God does not bring his justice through reforms introduced by the Pharaohs of this world.[13]

Why then does Church Theology appeal to the top rather than to the people who are suffering? Why does this theology not demand that the oppressed stand up for their rights and wage a struggle against their oppressors? Why does it not tell them that it is *their* duty to work for justice and to change the unjust structures? Perhaps the answer to these questions is that appeals from the "top" in the church tend very easily to be appeals to the "top" in society. An appeal to the conscience of those who perpetuate the system of injustice must be made. But real change and true justice can only come from below, from the people — most of whom are Christians.

3.3   Non-violence

The stance of Church Theology on non-violence, expressed as a blanket condemnation of all that is *called* violence, has not only been unable to curb the violence of our situation; it has actually, although unwittingly, been a major contributing factor in the recent escalation of State violence. Here again non-violence has been made into an absolute principle that applies to anything anyone *calls* violence without regard for who is using it, which side they are on, or what purpose they may have in mind. In our situation, this is simply counter-productive.

The problem for the church here is the way the word "violence" is being used in the propaganda of the State. The State and the media have chosen to call violence what some people do in the townships as they struggle for their liberation, i.e., throwing stones, burning cars and buildings, and sometimes killing collaborators. But this *excludes* the structural, institutional, and unrepentant violence of the State and especially the oppressive and naked violence of the police and the army. These things are not counted as violence. And even when they are acknowledged to be "excessive," they are called "misconduct" or even "atrocities" but never violence. Thus the phrase "violence in the townships" comes to mean what the young people are doing and not what the police are doing or what apartheid in general is doing to people. If one calls for non-violence in such circumstances one appears to be criticizing the resistance of the people while justifying or at least overlooking the violence of the police and the State. That is how it is understood not only by the State and its supporters but also by the people who are struggling for their freedom. Violence, especially in our circumstances, is a loaded word.

It is true that church statements and pronouncements do also condemn the violence of the police. They do say that they condemn *all violence*. But is it legitimate, especially in our circumstances, to use the same word "violence" in a blanket condemnation to cover the ruthless and repressive activities of the State and the desperate attempts of the people to defend themselves? Do such abstractions and generalizations not confuse the issue? How can acts of oppression, injustice, and domination be equated with acts of resistance and self-defense? Would it be legitimate to describe both the physical force used by a rapist and the physical force used by a woman trying to resist the rapist as violence?

Moreover, there is nothing in the Bible or in our Christian tradition that would permit us to make such generalizations. Throughout the Bible the word "violence" is used to describe everything that is done by a wicked oppressor (for example, Ps. 72:12–14; Isa. 59:1–8; Jer. 22:13–17; Amos 3:9–10; 6:3; Mic. 2:2; 3:1–3; 6:12). It is never used to describe the activities of Israel's armies in attempting to liberate themselves or to resist aggression. When Jesus says that we should turn the other cheek, he is telling us that we must not take revenge; he is not saying that we should never defend ourselves or others. There is a long and consistent Christian tradition about the use of physical force to defend oneself against aggressors and tyrants. In other words there are circumstances when physical force may be used. They are very restrictive circumstances, only as the very last resort and only as the lesser of two evils, or, as Bonhoeffer put it, "the lesser of two guilts." But it is simply not true to say that every possible use of physical force is violence and that no matter what the circumstances may be it is never permissible.

This is not to say that any use of force at any time by people who are oppressed is permissible simply because they are struggling for their liberation. There have been cases of killing and maiming that no Christian would want to approve of. But then our disapproval is based upon a concern for genuine liberation and a conviction that such acts are unnecessary, counter-productive, and unjustifiable, and not because they fall under a blanket condemnation of any use of physical force in any circumstances.

And finally what makes the professed non-violence of Church Theology extremely suspect in the eyes of very many people, including ourselves, is the tacit support that many church leaders give to the growing *militarization* of the South African State. How can one condemn all violence and then appoint chaplains to a very violent and oppressive army? How can one condemn all violence and then allow young white males to accept their conscription into the armed forces? Is it because the activities of the armed forces and the police are counted as defensive? That raises very serious questions about whose side such church leaders might be on. Why are the activities of young blacks in the townships not regarded as defensive?

The problem of the church here is that it starts from the premise that the apartheid regime in South Africa is a *legitimate authority*. It ignores the fact that it is a white minority regime which has imposed itself upon the majority of the people, that is, blacks, in this country and that it maintains itself by brutality and violent force and the fact that a majority of South Africans regard this regime as illegitimate.

In practice what one calls "violence" and what one calls "self-defense" seems to depend upon which side one is on. To call all physical force "violence" is to try to be neutral and to refuse to make a judgment about who is right and who is wrong. The attempt to remain neutral in this kind of conflict is futile. Neutrality enables the status quo of oppression (and therefore violence) to continue. It is a way of giving tacit support to the oppressor, a support for brutal violence.[14]

3.4   The Fundamental Problem

It is not enough to criticize Church Theology; we must also try to account for it. What is behind the mistakes and misunderstandings and inadequacies of this theology?

In the first place we can point to a lack of *social analysis*. We have seen how Church Theology tends to make use of absolute principles like reconciliation, negotiation, non-violence, and peaceful solutions and applies them indiscriminately and uncritically to all situations. Very little attempt is made to analyze what is actually happening in our society and why it is happening. It is not possible to make valid moral judgments about a society without first understanding that society. The analysis of apartheid that underpins Church Theology is simply inadequate. The present crisis has now made it very clear that the efforts of church leaders to promote effective and practical ways of changing our society have failed. This failure is due in no small measure to the fact that Church Theology has not developed a social analysis that would enable it to understand the mechanics of injustice and oppression.

Closely linked to this is the lack in Church Theology of an adequate understanding of politics and *political strategy*. Changing the structures of a society is fundamentally a matter of politics. It requires a political strategy based upon a clear social or political analysis. The church has to address itself to these strategies and to the analysis upon which they are based. It is into this political situation that the church has to bring the gospel. Not as an alternative solution to our problems as if the gospel provided us with a non-political solution to political problems. There is no specifically Christian solution. There will be a Christian way of approaching the political solutions, a Christian spirit and motivation and attitude. But there is no way of bypassing politics and political strategies.

But we have still not pinpointed the fundamental problem. Why has Church Theology not developed a social analysis? Why does it have an inadequate understanding of the need for political strategies? And why does it make a virtue of neutrality and sitting on the sidelines?

The answer must be sought in the *type of faith and spirituality* that has dominated church life for centuries. As we all know, spirituality has tended to be an otherworldly affair that has very little, if anything at all, to do with the affairs of this world. Social and political matters were seen as worldly affairs that have nothing to do with the spiritual concerns of the church. Moreover, spirituality has also been understood to be purely private and individualistic. Public affairs and social problems were thought to be beyond the sphere of spirituality. And finally the spirituality we inherit tends to rely upon God to intervene in his own good time to put right what is wrong in the world. That leaves very little for human beings to do except to pray for God's intervention.

It is precisely this kind of spirituality that, when faced with the present crisis in South Africa, leaves so many Christians and church leaders in a state of near paralysis.

It hardly needs saying that this kind of faith and this type of spirituality have no biblical foundation. The Bible does not separate the human person from the world in which he or she lives; it does not separate the individual from the social or one's private life from one's public life. God redeems the whole person as part of God's whole creation (Rom. 8:18–24). A truly biblical spirituality would penetrate into every aspect of human existence and would exclude nothing from God's redemptive will. Biblical faith is prophetically relevant to everything that happens in the world.

CHAPTER FOUR

TOWARD A PROPHETIC THEOLOGY

Our present *kairos* calls for a response from Christians that is biblical, spiritual, pastoral, and, above all, prophetic. *What is it then that would make our response truly prophetic? What would be the characteristics of a Prophetic Theology?*[15]

4.1 Prophetic Theology

To be truly prophetic, our response would have to be, in the first place, solidly grounded in the Bible. Our *kairos* impels us *to return to the Bible* and to search the Word of God for a message that is relevant to what we are experiencing in South Africa today. This will be no mere academic exercise. Prophetic Theology differs from academic theology because, whereas academic theology deals with all biblical themes in a systematic manner and formulates general Christian principles and doctrines, Prophetic Theology concentrates on those aspects of the Word of God that have an immediate bearing upon the critical situation in which we find ourselves. The theology of the prophets does not pretend to be comprehensive and complete, it speaks to the particular circumstances of a particular time and place — the *kairos*.

Consequently a prophetic response and a Prophetic Theology would include a *reading of the signs of the times*. This is what the great Biblical prophets did in their times and this is what Jesus tells us to do. When the Pharisees and Sadducees ask for a sign from heaven, he tells them to "read the signs of the times" (Matt. 16:3) or to "interpret this *kairos*" (Luke 12:56). A Prophetic Theology must try to do this. It must know what is happening, analyze what is happening (social analysis), and then interpret what is happening in the light of the gospel. This means that the starting point for Prophetic Theology will be our experience of the present *kairos,* our experience of oppression and tyranny, our experience of conflict, crisis, and struggle, our experience of trying to be Christians in this situation. It is with this in mind that we must begin to search the scriptures.

Another thing that makes Prophetic Theology different is that it is always a *call to action*. The prophets do not have a purely the-

oretical or academic interest in God and in the signs of the times.
They call for repentance, conversion, and change. They are critical, severely critical, of the status quo; they issue warnings about
God's punishment, and in the name of God they promise great
blessings for those who do change. Jesus did the same. "Repent,"
he says "the *kairos* has come and the Kingdom of God is close at
hand."

Thus prophecy is always *confrontational*. It confronts the evils
of the time and speaks out against them in no uncertain terms.
Prophetic Theology is not afraid to take a stand, clearly and un-
ambiguously. Prophetic statements are stark and simple without
being hedged in with qualifications or possible exceptions. They
deal with good and evil, justice and injustice, God and the devil.
It is not surprising then that any theology that is truly prophetic
will be controversial and in some circles it will be very unpopular.
The prophets were persecuted and Jesus was crucified.

Nevertheless, Prophetic Theology will place a great deal of emphasis upon *hope*. Despite all the criticisms, condemnations, and
warnings of doom, prophecy always has a message of hope for the
future. After death comes resurrection. That is the prophetic good
news.

A genuinely Prophetic Theology will also be deeply *spiritual*.
All its words and actions will have to be infused with a spirit
of fearlessness and courage, a spirit of love and understanding, a
spirit of joy and hope, a spirit of strength and determination. A
Prophetic Theology would have to have in it the mind of Christ,
his willingness to suffer and to die, his humility and his power, his
willingness to forgive and his anger about sin, his spirit of prayer
and of action.

Last but not least Prophetic Theology should be thoroughly
practical and *pastoral*. It will *denounce* sin and *announce* salvation.
But to be prophetic our theology must name the sins and the
evils that surround us and the salvation that we are hoping for.
Prophecy must name the sins of apartheid, injustice, oppression
and tyranny in South Africa today as "an offense against God"
and the measures that must be taken to overcome these sins and
the suffering that they cause. On the other hand prophecy will
announce the hopeful good news of future liberation, justice, and
peace, as God's will and promise, naming the ways of bringing this
about and encouraging people to take action.

4.2 Suffering and Oppression in the Bible[16]

Black Theology, African Theology, and the theology of the African Independent churches have already laid great emphasis upon the biblical teaching about suffering, especially the suffering of Jesus Christ. When we read the Bible from the point of view of our daily experience of suffering and oppression, then what stands out for us is the many, many vivid and concrete descriptions of suffering and oppression throughout the Bible culminating in the cross of Jesus Christ.

For most of their history from Exodus to Revelation, the people of the Bible suffered under one kind of oppression or another: "The sons of Israel are oppressed" (Jer. 50:33); "You will be exploited and crushed continually" (Deut. 28:33). They were oppressed by the tyrannical, imperial nations around them. First it was the Egyptians: "The Egyptians ill-treated us, they gave us no peace and inflicted harsh slavery upon us" (Deut. 26:6). Then the various Canaanite kings oppressed them, for example Jabin the Canaanite king of Hasor "cruelly oppressed the Israelites for twenty years" (Jud. 4:3). And so it carried on with the Philistines, the Assyrians, the Babylonians, the Greeks, and the Romans, each in turn exercising an oppressive domination over this small nation.

But this was not all. The people of Israel were also for many centuries oppressed *internally,* within their own country, by the rich and the powerful and especially by the kings or rulers of Israel who were for the most part typical oriental tyrants. "Here we are now, enslaved; here in the land you gave our Fathers, we are slaves. Its rich fruits swell the profit of the kings who dispose as they please of our bodies and our cattle" (Neh. 9:36–37). For the people of South Africa this situation is all too familiar.

The experience of oppression is vividly described in the Bible. First of all it is described as the painful experience of being crushed to the ground: "Yahweh, they crush your people" (Ps. 94:5); "we are bowed in the dust, our bodies crushed to the ground" (Ps. 44:25). It is the experience of being weighed down by heavy loads (Exod. 1:11; Matt. 11:28). But it is more than just an experience of being degraded and humiliated. They lived with the terrifying reality of killings and murders. "We are being massacred daily" (Ps. 44:22). "Yahweh, they oppress your hereditary people, murdering and massacring widows, orphans and migrants" (Ps. 94:5–6).

What grief and torment this causes. "My bones are in torment, my soul is in utter torment. I am worn out with groaning, every night I drench my pillow and soak my bed with tears, my eye is wasted with grief; I have grown old with enemies all round me" (Ps. 6:3, 6–10).

Their oppressors were their enemies. The people of Israel were in no doubt about that. There seemed to be no limit to the wickedness and sinfulness of these enemies: greed, arrogance, violence, and barbaric cruelty. "My enemies cluster round me, breathing hostility, entrenched in their fat, their mouths utter arrogant claims; now they are closing in. They look like lions eager to tear to pieces" (Ps. 17:9–12). "They [the rulers of Israel] have devoured the flesh of my people and torn off their skin and crushed their bones and shredded them like meat" (Micah 3:3).

Only people who had actually experienced oppression could have written such vivid and graphic descriptions of what it means to be oppressed. In South Africa today, in this our *kairos,* more than ever before the people of the townships can identify fully with these descriptions of suffering, oppression, and tyranny.

Nor should we think that this concern about oppression is confined to the Old Testament. In the time of Jesus the Jews were oppressed by the Romans, the great imperial superpower of those days. But what was far more immediate and far more pressing was the *internal oppression* of the poor and the ordinary people by the Herods, the rich, the chief priests and elders, the Sadducees and Pharisees. These were the groups who were experienced more immediately as oppressors. In one way or another they were puppets of the Romans and to a greater or lesser extent they collaborated in the oppression of the poor. Jesus calls Herod "that fox" (Luke 13:32). He pronounces "woes" upon the rich (Luke 6:24–26); he calls the Pharisees hypocrites, whited sepulchres, and a brood of vipers who lay heavy burdens upon the shoulders of the people and never lift a finger to relieve them (Matt. 23 passim). It was the chief priests and the elders who handed Jesus over to the Romans.

Throughout his life Jesus associated himself with the poor and the oppressed, and as the suffering (or oppressed) servant of Yahweh he suffered and died for us. "Ours were the sufferings he bore, ours the sorrows he carried" (Isa. 53:4). He continues to do so, even today.

4.3   Social Analysis

It is in the light of the biblical teaching about suffering, oppression, and tyranny that our Prophetic Theology must begin to analyze our *kairos* and read the signs of our times. Although it will not be possible to attempt a detailed social analysis or a complete reading of the signs of our times in this document, we must start with at least the broad outlines of an analysis of the conflict in which we find ourselves.

It would be quite wrong to see the present conflict as simply a racial war. The racial component is there but we are not dealing with two equal races or nations each with their own selfish group interests. The situation we are dealing with here is one of tyranny and oppression. We can therefore use the social categories that the Bible makes use of, namely, *the oppressor and the oppressed.*

What we are dealing with here, in the Bible or in South Africa today, is a social structure. The oppressors are the people who knowingly or unknowingly represent a sinful *cause* and unjust *interests*. The oppressed are people who knowingly or unknowingly represent the opposite *cause* and *interests,* the cause of justice and freedom. Structurally in our society these two causes are in conflict. The individuals involved may or may not realize this but the structural oppression that in South Africa is called apartheid will sooner or later bring the people involved into conflict.

On the one hand we have the interest of those who benefit from the status quo and who are determined to maintain it at any cost, even at the cost of millions of lives. It is in their interests to introduce a number of reforms in order to ensure that the system is not radically changed and that they can continue to benefit from it as they have done in the past. They benefit from the system because it favors them and enables them to accumulate a great deal of wealth and to maintain an exceptionally high standard of living. And they want to make sure that it stays that way even if some adjustments are needed.

On the other hand we have those who do not benefit in any way from the system the way it is now. They are treated as mere labor units, paid starvation wages, separated from their families by migratory labor, moved about like cattle and dumped in homelands to starve — and all for the benefit of a privileged minority. They have no say in the system and are supposed to be grateful for the concessions that are offered to them like crumbs. It is not in their interests to allow this system to continue even in some "reformed" or "revised" form. They are no longer prepared to be crushed, oppressed, and exploited. They are determined to change the system radically so that it no longer benefits only the privileged few. And they are willing to do this even at the cost of their own lives. What they want is justice for all, irrespective of race, color, sex, or status.

Each of the two sides can be further subdivided according to the different opinions people or groups have about the means and strategies to be used to maintain the system or the means and strategies to be used to change it. An almost infinite variety of opinion is possible here and much debate and discussion is needed, as long as one does not loose sight of the fundamental structural division between efforts to continue oppression even in a mitigated or changed form and efforts to do away with oppression in principle and in every form. There are two conflicting projects here and no compromise is possible. Either we have full and equal justice for all or we don't.

Prophetic Theology therefore faces us with this fundamental choice that admits of no compromises. Jesus did the same. He faced the people with the fundamental choice between God and money. "You cannot serve two masters" (Matt. 6:24). Once we have made our choice, once we have taken sides, then we can begin to discuss the morality and effectiveness of means and strategies. It is therefore not primarily a matter of trying to reconcile individual people but a matter of trying to change unjust structures so that people will not be pitted against one another as oppressor and oppressed.

This is our *kairos.* The structural inequality (political, social, and economic) expressed in discriminatory laws, institutions, and practices has led the people of South Africa into a virtual civil war and rebellion against tyranny.

4.4   Tyranny

According to our Christian tradition, based upon what we have already seen in the Bible, once it is established beyond doubt that a particular ruler is a tyrant or that a particular regime is tyrannical, it forfeits the moral right to govern and the people acquire the right to resist and to find the means to protect their own interests against injustice and oppression. In other words a tyrannical regime has no *moral legitimacy*. It may be the *de facto* government and it may even be recognized by other governments and therefore be the *de jure* or legal government. But if it is a tyrannical regime, it is, from a moral and a theological point of view, *illegitimate*.

There are indeed some differences of opinion in the Christian tradition about the means that might be used to replace a tyrant *but* there has not been any doubt about our Christian duty to refuse to cooperate with tyranny and to do whatever we can to remove it.

Of course everything hinges on the definition of a tyrant. At what point does a government become a tyrannical regime?

The traditional Latin definition of a tyrant is *hostis boni communis* — an enemy of the common good. The purpose of all government is the promotion of what is called the common good of the people governed. To promote the common good is to govern in the interests of, and for the benefit of, all the people. Many governments fail to do this at times. There might be this or that injustice done to some of the people. And such lapses would indeed have to be criticized. But occasional acts of injustice would not make a government into an enemy of the people, a tyrant.

To be enemy of the people a government would have to be hostile to the common good *in principle*. Such a government would be acting against the interests of the people as a whole and permanently. This would be clearest in cases where the very policy of a government is hostile towards the common good and where the government has a mandate to rule in the interests of some of the people rather than in the interests of all the people. Such a government would be in principle *irreformable*. Any reform that it might try to introduce would not be calculated to serve the common good but to serve the interests of the minority from whom it received its mandate.

A tyrannical regime cannot continue to rule for very long without becoming more and more violent. As the majority of the people begin to demand their rights and to put pressure on the tyrant, so will the tyrant resort more and more to desperate, cruel, gross, and ruthless forms of tyranny and repression. The reign of a tyrant always ends up as a reign or terror. It is inevitable because from the start the tyrant is an enemy of the common good.

That leaves us with the question of whether the present government of South Africa is tyrannical or not. There can be no doubt what the majority of the people of South Africa think. For them the apartheid regime is indeed the enemy of the people, and that is precisely what they call it: the enemy. In the present crisis, more than ever before, the regime has lost any legitimacy that it might have had in the eyes of the people. Are the people right or wrong?

Apartheid is a system whereby a minority regime elected by one small section of the population is given an explicit mandate to govern in the interests of, and for the benefit of, the white community. Such a mandate or policy is by definition hostile to the common good of all the people. In fact because it tries to rule in the exclusive interests of whites and not in the interests of all, it ends up ruling in a way that is not even in the interests of those whites. It becomes an enemy of all the people. A tyrant. A totalitarian regime. A reign of terror.

This also means that the apartheid minority regime is irreformable. We cannot expect the apartheid regime to experience a conversion or change of heart and totally abandon the policy of apartheid. It has no mandate from its electorate to do so. Any reforms or adjustments it might make would have to be done in the interests of those who elected it. Individual members of the government could experience a real conversion and repent but, if they did, they would simply have to follow this through by leaving a regime that was elected and put into power precisely because of its policy of apartheid.

And that is why we have reached the present impasse. As the oppressed majority becomes more insistent and puts more and more pressure on the tyrant by means of boycotts, strikes, uprisings. burnings, and even armed struggle, the more tyrannical will this regime become. On the one hand it will use repressive measures: detentions, trials, killings, torture, bannings, propaganda, states of emergency, and other desperate and tyrannical methods. And on the other hand it will introduce reforms that will always be unacceptable to the majority because all its reforms must ensure that the white minority remains on top.

A regime that is in principle the enemy of the people cannot suddenly begin to rule in the interests of all the people. It can only be replaced by another government — one that has been elected by the majority of the people with an explicit mandate to govern in the interests of all the people.

A regime that has made itself the enemy of the people has thereby also made itself the enemy of God. People are made in the image and likeness of God and whatever we do to the least of them we do to God (Matt. 25:40, 45).

To say that the State or the regime is the enemy of God is not to say that all those who support the system are aware of this. On the whole they simply do not know what they are doing. Many people have been blinded by the regime's propaganda. They are frequently quite ignorant of the consequences of their stance. However, such blindness does not make the State any less tyrannical or any less of an enemy of the people and an enemy of God.

On the other hand the fact that the State is tyrannical and an enemy of God is no excuse for hatred. As Christians we are called upon to love our enemies (Matt. 5:44). It is not said that we should not or will not have enemies or that we should not identify tyrannical regimes as indeed our enemies. But once we have identified our enemies, we must endeavor to love them. That is not always easy. But then we must also remember that the most loving thing we can do for *both* the oppressed *and* for our enemies who are oppressors is to eliminate the oppression, remove the tyrants from power, and establish a just government for the common good of *all the people*.

4.5 Liberation and Hope in the Bible

The Bible, of course, does not only *describe* oppression, tyranny, and suffering. The message of the Bible is that oppression is sinful and wicked, an offense against God. The oppressors are godless sinners and the oppressed are suffering because of the sins of their oppressors. But there is *hope* because Yahweh, the God of the Bible, will *liberate* the oppressed from their suffering and misery. "He will redeem their lives from exploitation and outrage" (Ps. 74:14). "I have seen the miserable state of my people in Egypt. I have heard their appeal to be free of their slave-drivers. I mean to deliver them out of the hands of the Egyptians" (Exod. 3:7).

Throughout the Bible God appears as the liberator of the oppressed: "For the plundered poor, for the needy who groan, now I will act, says Yahweh" (Ps. 12:5). God is not neutral. He does not attempt to reconcile Moses and Pharaoh, to reconcile the Hebrew slaves with their Egyptian oppressors, or to reconcile the Jewish people with any of their later oppressors. "You have upheld the justice of my cause . . . judging in favor of the orphans and exploited so that earthborn man [human beings] may strike fear no more. My enemies are in retreat, stumbling, perishing as you confront them. Trouble is coming to the rebellious, the defiled, the tyrannical city" (Ps. 9:4; 10:18; 9:3; Zeph. 3:1). Oppression is a crime and it cannot be compromised with, it must be done away with. "They [the rulers of Israel] will cry out to God. But he will not answer them. He will hide his face at that time because of all the crimes they have committed" (Micah 3:4). "God, who does what is right, is always on the side of the oppressed" (Ps. 103:6).

There can be no doubt that Jesus, the Son of God, also takes up the cause of the poor and the oppressed and identifies himself with their interests. When Jesus stood up in the synagogue at Nazareth to announce his mission he made use of the words of Isaiah:

The Spirit of the Lord has been given to me.
For he has anointed me.
He has sent me to bring the good news to the poor,
to proclaim liberty to captives and to the blind new sight,
to set the downtrodden free,
to proclaim the Lord's year of favor.

[Luke 4:18–19]

Not that Jesus is unconcerned about the rich and the oppressor. These he calls to repentance. At the very heart of the gospel of Jesus Christ and at the very center of all true prophecy is a message of hope. Jesus has taught us to speak of this hope as the coming of God's Kingdom. We believe that God is at work in our world turning hopeless and evil situations to good so that God's Kingdom may come and God's Will may be done on earth as it is in heaven. We believe that goodness and justice and love will triumph in the end and that tyranny and oppression cannot last forever. One day "all tears will be wiped away" (Rev. 7:17; 12:4) and "the lamb will lie down with the lion" (Isa. 11:6). True peace and true reconciliation are not only desirable, they are assured and guaranteed. This is our faith and our hope. We believe in and hope for the resurrection.

4.6 A Message of Hope

Nothing could be more relevant and more necessary at this moment of crisis in South Africa than the Christian message of hope. As the crisis deepens day by day, what both the oppressor and the oppressed can legitimately demand of the churches is a message of hope. Most of the oppressed people in South Africa today and especially the youth do have hope. They are acting courageously and fearlessly because they have a sure hope that liberation will come. Often enough their bodies are broken, but nothing can now break their spirit. But hope needs to be confirmed. Hope needs to be maintained and strengthened. Hope needs to be spread. The people need to hear it said again and again that God is with them and that "the hope of the poor is never brought to nothing" (Ps. 9:18).

On the other hand the oppressor and those who believe the propaganda of the oppressor are desperately fearful. They must be made aware of the diabolical evils of the present system and they must be called to repentance. "By what right do you crush my people and grind the face of the poor?" (Isa. 3:15). But they must also be given something to hope for. At present they have false hopes. They hope to maintain the status quo and their special privileges with perhaps some adjustments, and they fear any real alternative. But there is much more than that to hope for and nothing to fear. Can the Christian message of hope not help them in this matter?

A Prophetic Theology for our times will focus our attention on the future. What kind of future do the oppressed people of South Africa want? What kind of future do the political organizations of the people want? What kind of future does God want? And how, with God's help, are we going to secure that future for ourselves? We must begin to plan the future now but above all we must heed God's call to action to secure God's future for ourselves in South Africa.

There is hope. There is hope for all of us. But the road to that hope is going to be very hard and very painful. The conflict and the struggle will intensify in the months and years ahead. That is now inevitable — because of the intransigence of the oppressor. But God is with us. We can only learn to become the instruments of his peace even unto death. We must participate in the cross

of Christ if we are to have the hope of participating in his resurrection.

Why is it that this powerful message of hope has not been highlighted in Church Theology, in the statements and pronouncements
of church leaders? Is it because they have been addressing themselves to the oppressor rather than to the oppressed. Is it because
they do not want to encourage the oppressed to be too hopeful for
too much?

Now is the time to act — to act hopefully, to act with full confidence and trust in God.

CHAPTER FIVE

CHALLENGE TO ACTION

5.1   God Sides with the Oppressed

To say that the church must now take sides unequivocally and consistently with the poor and the oppressed is to overlook the fact that the majority of Christians in South Africa have already done so. By far the greater part of the church in South Africa is poor and oppressed. Of course it cannot be taken for granted that everyone who is oppressed has taken up their own cause and is struggling for their own liberation. Nor can it be assumed that all oppressed Christians are fully aware of the fact that their cause is God's cause. Nevertheless it remains true that the church is already on the side of the oppressed because that is where the majority of its members are to be found. This fact needs to be appropriated and confirmed by the church as a whole.

At the beginning of this document it was pointed out that the present crisis has highlighted the divisions in the church. We are a divided church precisely because not all the members of our churches have taken sides against oppression. In other words not all Christians have united themselves with God "who is always on the side of the oppressed" (Ps. 103:6). As far as the present crisis is concerned, there is only one way forward to church unity, and that is for those Christians who find themselves on the side of the oppressor or sitting on the fence, to cross over to the other side to be united in faith and action with those who are oppressed. Unity and reconciliation within the church itself is only possible around God and Jesus Christ, who are to be found on the side of the poor and the oppressed.

If this is what the church must become, if this is what the church as a whole must have as its project, how then are we to translate it into concrete and effective action?

5.2   Participation in the Struggle

Christians, if they are not doing so already, must quite simply participate in the struggle for liberation and for a just society. The campaigns of the people, from consumer boycotts to stayaways, need to be supported and encouraged by the church. Criticism will sometimes be necessary but encouragement and support will also be necessary. In other words the present crisis challenges the whole church to move beyond a mere "ambulance ministry" to a ministry of involvement and participation.[17]

5.3   Transforming Church Activities

The church has its own specific activities: Sunday services, communion services, baptisms, Sunday school, funerals, and so forth. It also has its specific way of expressing its faith and its commitment, that is, in the form of confessions of faith. All of these activities must be reshaped to be more fully consistent with a prophetic faith related to the *kairos* that God is offering us today. The evil forces we speak of in baptism must be named. We know what these evil forces are in South Africa today. The unity and sharing we profess in our communion services or Masses must be named. It is the solidarity of the people inviting all to join in the struggle for God's peace in South Africa. The repentance we preach must be named. It is repentance for our share of the guilt for the suffering and oppression in our country.

Much of what we do in our church services has lost its relevance to the poor and the oppressed. Our services and sacraments have been appropriated to serve the need of the individual for comfort and security. Now these same church activities must be reappropriated to serve the real religious needs of all the people and to further the liberating mission of God and the church in the world.

5.4   Special Campaigns

Over and above its regular activities the church would need to have special programs, projects, and campaigns because of the special needs of the struggle for liberation in South Africa today. But there is a very important caution here. The church must avoid becoming a "Third Force," a force between the oppressor and the oppressed.[18] The church's programs and campaigns must not duplicate what the people's organizations are already doing, and, even more seriously, the church must not confuse the issue by having programs that run counter to the struggles of those political organizations that truly represent the grievances and demands of the people. Consultation, coordination, and cooperation will be needed. We all have the same goals even when we differ about the final significance of what we are struggling for.

5.5 Civil Disobedience

Once it is established that the present regime has no moral legitimacy and is in fact a tyrannical regime, certain things follow for the church and its activities. In the first place *the church cannot collaborate with tyranny*. It cannot or should not do anything that appears to give legitimacy to a morally illegitimate regime. Secondly, the church should not only pray for a change of government; it should also mobilize its members in every parish to begin to think and work and plan for a change of government in South Africa. We must begin to look ahead and begin working now with firm hope and faith for a better future. And finally the moral illegitimacy of the apartheid regime means that the church will have to be involved at times in *civil disobedience*. A church that takes its responsibilities seriously in these circumstances will sometimes have to confront and to disobey the State in order to obey God.

5.6 Moral Guidance

The people look to the church, especially in the midst of our present crisis, for moral guidance. In order to provide this the church must first make its stand absolutely clear and never tire of explaining and dialoguing about it. It must then help people to understand their rights and their duties. There must be no misunderstanding about the *moral duty* of all who are oppressed to resist oppression and to struggle for liberation and justice. The church will also find that at times it does need to curb excesses and to appeal to the consciences of those who act thoughtlessly and wildly.

But the church of Jesus Christ is not called to be a bastion of caution and moderation. The church should challenge, inspire, and motivate people. It has a message of the cross that inspires us to make sacrifices for justice and liberation. It has a message of hope that challenges us to wake up and to act with hope and confidence. The church must preach this message not only in words and sermons and statements but also through its actions, programs, campaigns, and divine services.

CONCLUSION

As we said in the beginning, there is nothing final about this document nor even about this second edition. Our hope is that it will continue to stimulate discussion, debate, reflection, and prayer, but, above all, that it will lead to action. We invite all committed Christians to take this matter further, to do more research, to develop the themes we have presented here, or to criticize them and to return to the Bible, as we have tried to do, with the question raised by the crisis of our times.

Although the document suggests various modes of involvement, it does not prescribe the particular actions anyone should take. We call upon all those who are committed to this prophetic form of theology to use the document for discussion in groups, small and big, to determine an appropriate form of action, depending on their particular situation, and to take up the action with other related groups and organizations.

The challenge to renewal and action that we have set out here is addressed to the church. But that does not mean that it is intended only for church leaders. The challenge of the faith and of our present *kairos* is addressed to all who bear the name Christian. None of us can simply sit back and wait to be told what to do by our church leaders or by anyone else. We must all accept responsibility for acting and living out our Christian faith in these circumstances. We pray that God will help all of us to translate the challenge of our times into action.

We, as theologians (both lay and professional), have been greatly challenged by our own reflections, our exchange of ideas, and our discoveries as we met together in smaller and larger groups to prepare this document or to suggest amendments to it. We are convinced that this challenge comes from God and that it is addressed to all of us. We see the present crisis, or *kairos,* as indeed a divine visitation.

And finally we also like to repeat our call to our Christian brothers and sisters throughout the world to give us the necessary support in this regard so that the daily loss of so many young lives may be brought to a speedy end.

EXPLANATORY NOTES

Chapter One

1. *Kairos* is the Greek word that is used in the Bible to designate a special moment of time when God visits his people to offer them a unique opportunity for repentance and conversion, for change and decisive action. It is a time of judgment. It is a moment of truth, a crisis (see, for example: Mark 1:15; 13:33; Luke 8:13; 19:44; Rom. 13:11–13; 1 Cor. 7:29; 1 Cor. 6:2; Tit. 1:3; Rev. 1:3; 22:10).

2. What is said here of Christianity and the church could be applied, *mutatis mutandis,* to other faiths and religions in South Africa; but this particular document is addressed to "all who bear the name Christian" (see Conclusion).

3. See Chapter Four of the Kairos Document, pp. 25–36 in this volume.

4. If the apostle Paul judged that the truth of the gospel was at stake when Greek and Jewish Christians no longer ate together (Gal. 2:11–14), how much more acute is the crisis for the gospel of Jesus Christ when some Christians take part in the systematic *oppression* of other Christians!

5. Matt. 12:25; 1 Cor. 1:13.

6. These are obviously not the only theologies that are current in South Africa but they represent the three Christian theological stances in relation to the present situation in South Africa.

Chapter Two

7. What we are referring to here is something more than the "Apartheid Theology" of the White Dutch Reformed churches that once tried to justify apartheid by appealing to certain texts in the Bible. Our analysis of present-day theological stances has led us to the conclusion that there is a State Theology that does not only justify racism but justifies all the activities of the State in its attempts to hold on to power and that is subscribed to as a theology well beyond the White Dutch Reformed churches.

8. This and all other quotations in this document are taken from the Jerusalem Bible. The reader is invited to compare this translation with others that he or she might prefer.

9. Oscar Cullmann, *The State in the New Testament* (London: SCM, 1957), p. 56.

10. For example: E. Käsemann, *Commentary on Romans* (London: SCM, 1980), pp. 354–357; O. Cullmann, *The State in the New Testament,* pp. 55–57.

Chapter Three

11. We realize only too well that we are making broad and sweeping generalizations here. There are some church statements that would be exceptions to this general tendency. However, what concerns us here is that there is a set of opinions that in the mind of the people is associated with the liberal English-speaking churches.

12. It should be noted here that there is a difference between the willingness to forgive, on the one hand, and the reality of forgiveness or the experience of being forgiven with all its healing consequences, on the other hand. God's forgiveness is unconditional and permanent in the sense that he is always

willing to forgive. Jesus expresses this on the cross by saying, "Father forgive them for they know not what they do" (Luke 23:24). However, we as sinners will not experience God's forgiveness in our lives, we will not actually be freed or liberated from our sins until we confess and renounce our sins (1 John 1:8–9) and until we demonstrate the fruits of repentance (Luke 3:7–14).

Human beings must also be *willing to forgive* one another at all times even seventy times seven times. But forgiveness will not become a reality with all its healing effects until the offender repents. Thus in South Africa forgiveness will not become an experienced reality until the apartheid regime shows signs of genuine repentance. Our willingness to forgive must not be taken to mean a willingness to allow sin to continue, a willingness to allow our oppressors to continue oppressing us. To ask us to forgive our unrepentant oppressors in the sense that we simply ignore or overlook the fact that they are continuing to humiliate, crush, repress, imprison, maim, and kill us is to add insult to injury.

What is required at this stage above all else is repentance and conversion.

13. Despite what is clearly stated here in the text, several commentators have interpreted the concept of "justice from below" as an exclusion of God and an exclusion of the people who are now at the top. This misinterpretation is very revealing. In the first place it assumes that *God belongs on top* together with the kings, rulers, governments, and others who have power, whether they are oppressors or not, and that God cannot work *from below*, through the efforts of the people who are oppressed. It assumes that God is on the side of the oppressor (on top) and not on the side of the oppressed (below). This is precisely what the Kairos Document is contesting.

In the second place there is the conclusion that "justice from below" excludes the white community and anyone else who is presently on top. This is based upon the very revealing assumption that conversion and repentance are impossible and that those who are presently on top will never climb down in order to negotiate as equals with those who are presently at the bottom. Unless they do this, they will indeed be unable to be part of the construction of a just and peaceful South Africa. Those who refuse to repent and change cannot become instruments of God's justice and God's peace.

14. What we have said here about violence and non-violence does not pretend to be a solution to the complex moral problems that we are all faced with as our country is plunged more and more deeply into civil war. Our only aim in this section has been to critique an oversimplified and misleading theology of non-violence.

Chapter Four

15. Many readers of the first edition suggested that the meaning of Prophetic Theology should be spelled out more clearly. The characteristics of Prophetic Theology that have been included in this second edition are a summary of discussions among Kairos theologians both before and immediately after the publication of the first edition.

It should also be noted that there is a subtle difference between Prophetic Theology and people's theology. The Kairos Document itself, signed by theologians, ministers, and other church workers, and addressed to all who bear the name Christian, is a prophetic statement. But the process that led to the production of the document, the process of theological reflection and action in groups, the involvement of many different people in doing theology, was an exercise in people's theology. The document is therefore pointing out two things: that our present *kairos* challenges church leaders and others Christians to speak out prophetically and that our present *kairos* is challenging all of us to do theology together reflecting upon our experiences in working for justice and peace in South Africa and thereby developing together a better theological understanding of our *kairos*. The method that we used to produce the Kairos Document shows that theology is not the preserve of professional theologians, ministers, and priests. Ordinary Christians can participate in theological reflection and should be encouraged to do so. When this people's theology is proclaimed to others to challenge and inspire them, it takes on the character of a Prophetic Theology.

16. This section has been rewritten mainly because of the request that more quotations from the Bible be included in the text.

Chapter Five

17. However, the church must participate in the struggle as a *church* and not as a political organization. Individual Christians as citizens of this country can and must join the political organizations that are struggling for justice and liberation, but the church as church must not become a political organization or subject itself to the dictates of any political party. The church has its own motivation, its own inspiration for participating in the struggle for justice and peace. The church has its own beliefs and its own values that impel it to become involved, alongside of other organizations, in God's cause of liberation for the oppressed. The church will have its own way of operating and it may sometimes have its own special programs and campaigns, but it does not have, and cannot have, its own political blueprint for the future, its own political policy, because the church is not a political party. It has another role to play in the world.

The individual Christian, therefore, is both a member of the church and a member of society, and, on both accounts, Christians should be involved in doing what is right and just. The same is no doubt true of people who adhere to other religious faiths.

18. There has been a lot of debate about whether the church should be a "Third Force" or not. It is closely related to the question of whether the church should take sides or not, which we explained in the previous note. The whole question and the full debate will be dealt with in a forthcoming book entitled *The Kairos Debate*.

Frank Chikane

"This was a people's document..."

— KAIROS DOCUMENT, Preface

The methodology used in producing the Kairos Document is of vital importance in understanding the document itself.

During May 1985, we published an issue of *ICT (Institute of Contextual Theology) News,* which is usually published once a quarter. We felt that the nature of the crisis had superseded the publication that we had at the printers. We felt that it was not going to address the urgency of the crisis as we found it and saw it during that time. There was a big struggle in the ICT office. Some felt we should publish a special issue of the *ICT News,* but there was also some resistance because this would involve a lot of work. In the end we decided to go ahead with the special issue.

We soon discovered that even after four years of work in the Institute we still thought in the traditional way about doing theology. We wanted to write about the experiences of the people rather than have the people reflect on their own experience. We felt that we needed to go to the people and reflect with them on their experiences and listen to what they were saying. It is out of that crisis that the Kairos Document came.

We had the first meeting with a number of people in Soweto to reflect on the situation. At that time we had no Kairos Document in our minds at all. In time we discovered that we were dealing

---

Frank Chikane is the former director of the Institute of Contextual Theology and is currently Secretary of the South African Council of Churches. This is an edited version of his address to the Kairos Covenant meeting in Chicago, November 1986.

with something more serious than the *ICT News* in itself. We decided that the *ICT News* would carry out its own theme coming out of this discussion, but that we were dealing with something else now, that is, the way in which the church has to respond to the crisis in our situation.

People are speculating about who wrote this document. They look at the list at the end of the document and they say it doesn't happen like that. No hundred and fifty-two people can produce such a document. There must have been a conspiracy of one or two or a few people. Some group in South Africa said seven communists drafted the document and got everybody else to sign it. At first I didn't know where they found the figure of seven. Later I discovered that the first people who met to discuss the crisis decided that we couldn't discuss anything because we were only seven. So we decided to call another meeting. I'm sure they got their information from the security police that there were seven people in that first discussion.

Who are the authors of the document? Different people wrote different notes at different times. At times we mandated that certain people write about what the people were saying about a particular issue. They would go back with their traditional material that they produced in their own way and present it to the people, and they were rejected. There were packages of materials that we had to file away because people just said, "You have now started talking the language that we don't understand. We are not interested in that. Your word 'eschatology' has nothing to do with us. We want to understand what we are talking about, and you theologians come with terms to keep us busy debating about concepts without getting involved in dealing with the system."

As a result we together came out with a document that no one of us would have produced. If I had a chance I would have written a document different from the document we have today. I think it was Dr. Goba who said, "If I had written that document, I would not have used the word 'devil' the way they've used it here." We had a heavy argument about the word, and the people in the townships said, "Ka si, Sotho ki Santani" (This system is a Satan). They were trying to express their idea in the language they use in the streets. They were saying, "This is a devil and we must deal with it." The development of the document came out of the people's experiences, the people's struggles, the people's pain. And most of the theologians who participated in this process learned professionally a great deal during this process.

Theology must be a by-product of the process. I like looking at the Bible as an afterthought; the written word that we call the Bible is an afterthought. People write about things that have happened; they write about particular experiences. Reflection on experience in faith becomes the word of God. This document is actually a by-product of a process, the process of struggle to remove the apartheid regime. That is the issue, not the document per se.

The action is the issue rather than the theoretical reflection. We reflected on the praxis of the church itself and realized that something was wrong. You need to think more of action than of theory, and reflect on the action to get your theory. You must say, What are we going to do? You must have an intention. My criticism of the sanctions debates and the decisions made on sanctions by some Western governments that say, "They won't work," is that they have no intention of making them work. They've not made a decision that they want to remove apartheid. And if they don't make a decision, they will make sure sanctions do not work. You must begin by making a decision: I am going to make sure that apartheid goes.

During our treason trial we were asked, what do you mean "getting rid of apartheid"? Does it mean you overthrow the government? That constitutes treason. We are going to need to get rid of the apartheid system. You cannot get rid of it unless you start from the premise that the apartheid regime is illegitimate.

I think the church has failed in history. The church theologizes about things, but it doesn't begin to make sure that its theology makes a difference; it doesn't act. It makes resolutions. It has a library of resolutions. As long as some church people adopt a resolution and pack it away, they satisfy themselves. The Kairos Document says that you must start from the premise that this government is illegitimate and must go.

The South African situation is characterized by what I call primary sin and secondary sin. When they came to our country, for instance, the Western missionaries were concerned with secondary sin. Today the church is expected to worry about the drunkards and the fornicators and the violent people and those immoral people in the townships. And it shouldn't worry about the person who commits the primary sin that creates those results.

What I'm dealing with in the township is the secondary sin. The primary sin is actually elsewhere. The thieves I have to preach to are actually products of the primary thieves on the factory floor where they are robbed, where they are underpaid. And when they begin to steal, then I have to preach to them and say don't steal. But the real thief is the one who owns suits, who sits in hotels, who sits in comfortable places.

Sin has eluded the church. It has become sophisticated. It has gone into quarters where the church cannot penetrate. And as the result, we have seen the victims at the end, and the church focuses on the victims rather than the primary sinners. The primary people who benefit from that system are not aware of this reality. Or if they are aware, they are deliberately ignoring it.

Every soul that is killed by the apartheid regime dies so that somebody elsewhere can benefit. Every comfort elsewhere is at the expense of our people. You must begin by asking what is the sin of your community that is causing the pain of the people in South Africa.

I have to work with people who are oppressed and want to be liberated. Your job is more difficult. You have to work with people who are privileged, who are enjoying their lives, who know that any decision has to do with their livelihood, with their privilege, with their comfort. That might be more of an uphill struggle than you thought.

Part Two

STATE THEOLOGY

Richard J. Mouw

*"The concern of Christians is...
a just law and a right order...."*

— KAIROS DOCUMENT, 2.2

Those South African people — governmental leaders and their supporters — who have taken it upon themselves to defend the laws and practices and attitudes associated with the program of "separate development" have in fact often based their case on a discernible theological perspective. What is that perspective? What is wrong with it? And what can we as Christians in North America learn from the way in which the Kairos Document critically evaluates that theological perspective?

A decade or so ago the South African writer W. A. de Klerk published a book entitled *Puritans in Africa,* in which he discussed Afrikaner civil religion. As the title suggests, de Klerk drew a parallel between the Afrikaner and the Puritan understandings of cultural mission. Just as the Puritans who came to the shores of this North American continent viewed themselves as the New Israel, called, like Israel of old, to pass through a wilderness experience that would culminate in the establishment of a righteous nation that would serve as a light to the nations, so also the people who gradually came to realize their identity as the Afrikaner nation have thought of themselves as fulfilling a divine mandate in Southern Africa.

Now, as some of us know, scholars in South Africa have been debating the question in recent years of how religious the early

Richard J. Mouw is Professor of Christian Philosophy and Ethics at Fuller Theological Seminary, Pasadena, Calif.

generations of white settlers in Southern Africa really were. But whether or not those early folks actually thought of themselves as engaged in some sort of divine mission, there can be no doubt that later generations came to tell the *story* of the past in that manner. If anything, then, the self-understanding of the Afrikaner people has become over the years more and more explicit in its theological tone, so that in the twentieth century many people in the government of South Africa have operated with a rather overt and detailed theology of chosen-people-hood.

A good case can be made for the view that the reverse pattern has occurred in the United States. A number of people have argued — and I am thinking here especially of the kind of case made by Robert Jewett in his book *The Captain America Complex* — that the experience of the American nation began with a rather clear and explicit Puritan theology of chosen-people-hood, but that in the course of our history that theology got submerged and repackaged in more secularized terms. Thus a Dean Rusk or a Henry Kissinger or a George Shultz doesn't operate with a clear theology of the messianic role of the American nation — although such folks often presuppose an understanding of a special national *calling,* or an international *mission,* that is itself an unconscious legacy from the overt theology of the Puritans.

I mention these matters in order to illustrate my contention that thinking seriously about the State Theology of the Afrikaner people can be for us in North America a very helpful exercise in self-understanding, even as it can also be — to be sure — an important means of discerning what the Lord is calling us to do by way of supporting the struggle for justice in the southern portion of the African continent. And I am convinced that we need all the help we can get in gaining theological self-understanding with regard to our own relationship to human government. Many of our black Christian sisters and brothers from South Africa have been known to observe that we North American Christians don't always seem very aware of the need to do our theological homework when it comes to dealing with political questions. I am convinced that they are correct in that assessment. I am also convinced that the Kairos Document points us to the way in which biblically-grounded theological reflection can take place in the midst of the struggle for justice, righteousness, and peace. And the hope that we as North Americans can learn from the Kairos Document is even more greatly enhanced by the fact that, as I have suggested, the State Theology that has often been explicitly formulated and defended on South African soil has strong ties of kinship to the more submerged and less consciously articulated theological perspective that has had such a formative influence in the development of American political thought and practice.

It is with that hope, that we all have much to learn from a serious wrestling with the theological content of the Kairos Document, that I want to point here to three closely-related elements in the document's brief discussion of the State Theology of South Africa.

Loyalty to Tradition

The first element is the way in which the document appeals to the tradition of Christian orthodoxy in making its case. This is an important factor to point to in the context of our North American discussion of these matters. Some of us were present at a recent one-day conference on South Africa that the State Department sponsored for "religious leaders." At that conference we heard a well-known American theologian express some brief, but negative, comments about the Kairos Document. One remark in particular deserves careful scrutiny. He said, as I put it down in my notes: "Like liberation theology, the Kairos Document makes disobedience to government a test of Christian discipleship."

That is an unfortunate and misleading comparison. Whether intended or not, its effect was to facilitate a facile, and I think cavalier, dismissal of the important message of the Kairos Document. I certainly have no desire here to engage in polemics against liberation theology — or more accurately, liberation theolo*gies* — since I have benefited much from my own wrestling with the theological literature that is associated with that label. But I think it is important for me to emphasize here that I do not consider myself to be a liberation theologian. I would like to make it as clear as I can that the question of whether we should agree with what is said in the Kairos Document is a different question from whether we agree with liberation theology.

"Like liberation theology, the Kairos Document makes disobedience to government a test of Christian discipleship." As a conservative Calvinist I resent that attempt to cloud the issues by associating the Kairos Document with views that constitute, in the

minds of many church leaders who attend State Department brief-
ings, sufficient grounds for an instant dismissal of the document's
line of argument. In article 36 of the Belgic Confession, a binding
confessional document in my Dutch Reformed tradition — binding
also in the Dutch Reformed churches of South Africa — Christians
are urged to submit to the authority of civil magistrates. But that
required submission is not portrayed in an unqualified manner.
Rather the writers of the Belgic Confession insist that Christians
are to obey magistrates "in all things which are not repugnant to
the Word of God."

This is the real issue. And it cannot be avoided by glib attempts to portray the Kairos Document as a partisan-political or
ideologically-radical manifesto. One might just as well as say something like this: "Like liberation theology, the writers of the Belgic
Confession — or the French Huguenots or John Knox or the Scot-
tish Covenanters or St. Thomas or St. Augustine and Marsiglio of
Padua and Phoebe Palmer and Catherine Booth — made disobedience to unjust government a test of Christian discipleship." The
fact is that it is difficult to find any group of Christians who do
not think that we must refuse to obey those governments whose
policies are, in the words of the Belgic Confession, "repugnant to
the Word of God." That is not really a matter of serious debate
in the Christian tradition. The real issue with reference to South
Africa is whether the racist policies and laws of the present government are and ought to be repugnant to those who have heard
the gospel's joyful sound. I believe that they are *deeply* repugnant.
And I believe that the authors of the Kairos Document stand in
the mainstream of the Christian tradition when they make their
case in response to the repugnant theology of the South African
status quo.

And I don't think that I am simply adding my own conservative-
evangelical gloss here to a document that presupposes a very different framework from the one I am employing. For one thing, it is
worth noting the fact that the word "heresy" appears many times
in this Kairos Document. This body of witnesses in South Africa
has succeeded in reintroducing the word "heresy" as a tool of serious theological assessment in mainstream ecumenical discussion.
And it is also interesting to note that while the Kairos group does
not quote extensively from theological sources, in the one document in the Kairos literature that includes footnotes — the theo-

logical rationale included in the June 16, 1985, call to prayer — the fourteen citations of supporting literature include one reference to Tertullian, one to Augustine, one to St. Thomas, one to Martin Luther, one to Abram Kuyper, two to Karl Barth, two to John Calvin, and four to papal documents. Hardly a display of theological and political leftism!

Rendering to Caesar

The second element is the way the Kairos Document, in its solid and creative appropriation of the theological traditions, rightly instructs us regarding the need to relativize the claims of existing governments. The Kairos writers correctly insist that the biblical call to submit to the authority of the State is misunderstood and misused when it is taken, as is the case in State Theology, as legitimizing "an attitude of blind obedience and absolute servility towards the State." The Kairos Document's discussion of Romans 13 is helpful in this regard. And it addresses matters that are of great importance for the North American Christian community.

For the past twenty years I have been conducting my own private, and admittedly less than fully scientific, survey on such issues. As someone who has had many opportunities to talk with very diverse Christian groups about the Christian obligations to those who possess political authority, I have discovered that those Christians who think that the Bible urges us to be passive and subservient toward those who occupy offices of political authority — that those Christians operate, for the most part, with no more than three biblical proof texts in their theological arsenal. The first is the one discussed in the Kairos Document: Romans 13:1–7, where the apostle refers to the powers-that-be as "ordained" by God. The other two are the "Render unto Caesar" passage, quoted by all three Synoptic writers, and Jesus' comment to Pilate, in John 18:36, that his "kingship is not of this world."

The insistence of the Kairos writers that Romans 13 must be understood in its context, as well as in its relationship to the rest of the biblical record, is crucial for understanding all such texts. For example, many people cite Jesus' comment to Pilate without attending to the events that immediately follow. They fail to grasp the fact that, for example, Jesus challenged Pilate's political authority in a very concrete way on Easter Sunday morning. The

Resurrection was illegal. It was the first act of Christian civil disobedience. Pilate sealed the tomb and put a squadron of soldiers in the garden to keep the stone from being rolled away. When Jesus burst forth from the tomb and struck down the soldiers, he was offering an important clarification of his statement to Pilate. *Whatever* Jesus meant when he told Pilate that his kingship was not of the order of this world, and *whatever* he meant when he told the Pharisees that God wants us to render to Caesar what belongs to Caesar — *whatever* Jesus meant, he was not granting to Pilate or to Caesar the authority to cancel the Resurrection.

Similarly, to be consistent with the many popular readings of Romans 13, the kind of reading that is central to the State Theology of South Africa, one would expect a very different response from St. Peter when the angel came to deliver him from prison, as recorded in the book of Acts. One would expect him to say, "Get behind me, you messenger of Satan. Put the key back, and go away, and leave me alone. The powers that be are ordained of God; they are ministers of God for our good, rewarding those who do good and punishing those who do evil. Go away — for we must be subject for the Lord's sake to every human institution." But that was not the response. The apostles knew that civil authorities regularly stepped beyond the boundaries that God ordained for them, attempting to contain and control the work of the church of Jesus Christ. And they knew that the ministering angels were sent, in such situations — as they had been sent on Easter Sunday morning — to liberate and empower the church for faithfulness to the gospel of the Lamb who was slain.

The Kairos writers point us in the right direction when they insist that Romans 13 cannot be wrenched out of the larger biblical context that also includes the vision of Revelation 13, where the people of the Lamb refuse to submit to the authority of a government that has become beastly. Those faithful saints in John's vision know that the apostolic witness does not require them to engage in blind submission to that which is ungodly and repugnant to the divine Word. These various themes are brought together nicely in 1 Peter 2, which is perhaps the most detailed teaching passage on this subject in the apostolic writings. There the people of God are instructed to maintain "good conduct" in the larger society — but not simply by the kind of good works that will be *called* "good conduct" by the powers that be. Rather, they must do those things that will glorify God on the day of visitation. In that same passage Christians are urged to honor those who are the civil authorities; but they are at the same time told to honor all human beings, while loving the church and fearing the Lord. The Kairos Document rightly insists that the New Testament witness does not permit us to offer blind obedience to the civil authorities. We owe them honor — but no *more* than honor. We certainly do not owe them the "fear" that we must offer only to that God who alone is worthy of our worship and absolute obedience.

Government Ministry

The third element is the way in which the Kairos Document, in its loyalty to the traditions and its insistence upon the need to relativize the claims of governmental authorities, formulates its critique in the light of a biblical grasp of the proper and necessary "ministry" of government. This is a very important emphasis for North Americans to take seriously, since we often carry on our debates regarding "big" versus "small" government, or "strong" versus "weak" government, or "active" versus "minimal" government, as if the only relevant categories were pragmatic ones.

When the Kairos Document insists upon relativizing the claims of the South African government it does not simply do so out of some vague conviction that no human authority can be viewed with absolute seriousness, since we are all, after all, finite and frail. What is wrong with the South African government from the perspective of the Kairos Document is not simply that that government fails to recognize that it is only human. Rather, that government has failed in a different way: it has refused to live up to the very positive and clear divine requirement that governments do the work of justice.

To put it in slightly different terms: the proper application of Romans 13 to the South African situation does not consist in saying simply that State Theology fails to see that Romans 13 needs to be balanced off by texts like Revelation 13. Rather, the point is that State Theology is based on an improper understanding of Romans 13 itself. For there the Apostle is pointing to the way in which civil authorities, if they are to function in the way God intended, are required to fill a kind of "ministerial" function. And this function is specified, right in the text itself, with reference to some rather clear categories: governments, as ministers of God, are required to reward those who do good and to punish those who do evil.

If there were nothing else in the whole Bible about the role of government, this passage, Romans 13 itself, alone would be significant to expose the present South Africa regime for the unjust government, the disobedient minister, that it is. For its consistent policy has been to reward those who do *evil* and to *punish* those who do good. As the Kairos writers clearly and poignantly observe: "It is indeed the duty of the State to maintain law and order, but it has no divine mandate to maintain any kind of law and order.... The concern of Christians is that we should have in our country a just law and a right order" (2.2).

In my own recent studies of the development of Calvinist views of political authority in the Netherlands and Scotland I have been impressed by the way in which early Reformed writers regularly refer to the role of government in terms of nurturing images. Given the strong patriarchy of that tradition, for example, it is surprising to me how often the image of the ruler as a nursing mother is employed — probably an explicit reference to, among other passages, that marvelous verse in Isaiah 60 where God's people are promised that they shall someday suck the breast of kings.

The desire for a government that nurtures and feeds us is deeply rooted in the biblical vision. It shows up over and over again in the life of Israel, where the people prayed for a righteous ruler whose policies would make the hearts of the poor glad and whose judgments would be like rain falling upon the newly mowed grass (Psalm 72). It is expressed in the deep yearning for a kind of leadership that would feed the flock like a shepherd and where the little ones would be cradled in the royal arms and where those who are with young would be led gently by the hand.

It is in the light of this biblical vision that we must judge the South African government to be a ministerial failure; for it has cast the righteous into prisons, it has gunned down its children in the streets, it has harassed those who mourn, it has destroyed the meager habitations of the poor, it has turned a deaf ear to the cries of the widow and the orphan, and it has piled burden upon burden on the backs of those who are already bowed down under the yoke of oppression. One does not have to be a liberation theologian to say, as the Kairos Document says so clearly, that such a government has failed to be a minister of the God of the Scriptures.

The tragedy is compounded by the fact, of course, that this government claims to be an instrument of Christian orthodoxy. But those claims must be tested against the Scriptures, where we find the prophet Daniel, for example, stating the requirements of political orthodoxy in those minimal terms that God imposes even on the ruler of a professedly pagan nation: "Hear my words, O king, and let my counsel be acceptable to you: break off from your sins by practicing righteousness, and break off from your iniquities by showing mercy to the oppressed, that there may perhaps be a lengthening of your tranquility" (4:27). Those are, I say, the minimal standards of godly rule, whether applied to professedly Christian or to pagan governments. By those clear standards the South African government has failed to be the kind of minister described in Romans 13. And we must not be afraid to say that. Nor must we be afraid to remind our own governmental leaders of the basic requirements of godly rule, lest we fail to speak those words that are so necessary to hear if we are to experience a lengthening of our own tranquility.

James E. Hug, S.J.

*"State Theology ... needs to have
its own concrete symbol of evil...."*

—Kairos Document, 2.3

Our government, in attempting to link the Kairos Document to liberation theology, is trying to link it with Marxism and communism (see above p. 52). In our current cultural context, that is equivalent to painting it with the brush of all evil to discredit it. It is to use the label "communist" in the same way the South African government is using it. We must keep in mind that our current administration is headed by the president who referred to the Soviet Union as the "Evil Empire." Symbolizing communism as the embodiment of all evil sets it over against us and allows us to see ourselves, uncritically, as the symbol of goodness, of democratic Judeo-Christian values in the world.

I believe that President Reagan's Teflon character is due, at least in part, to the fact that the American people need to hear the message that we are good. Recall some of the major events of the last twenty-five years: the Vietnam war, the Civil Rights movement, the Women's movement, Watergate, the OPEC-generated economic crises. The people of this nation have been hit again and again with the message: "You are not who you thought you were. Your actions contradict your proudest ideals. You are not the special Chosen People of God you like to think you are!" President Reagan has ridden to power proclaiming "Yes we are! Our

James E. Hug, S.J., is Director of Research at the Center of Concern, Washington, D.C.

enemies are the evil ones. We can be Number One again. We are the Chosen People of God!"

In reaffirming that image, he is offering a soothing touch to a very crippled and injured national psyche. He is providing the false prophecy that people want to hear. That is an important part of his power.

But there is a twist to his prophecy, a twist to the way he presents the U.S. as a Chosen People. What he is saying on the surface is probably not what he really means beneath the surface.

The testimony of secretary of state George Shultz before Congress in July 1986, on the U.S. approach to South Africa, provides a clue to this twist. It includes this very interesting comment:

> I think there is some merit to the argument that the message delivered by the marketplace is a more powerful and deeper message than a message that might be delivered by some action that would be taken here [in Congress]. If you impose a political sanction, you are, in effect, saying that there is capital and business and everything that is just dying to get in here and take advantage of those opportunities, and you are going to stop it from doing so. It is more devastating to realize that without any such interposition capital is not coming; capital is leaving, and the economy is in a rapid downward spiral. That is a very powerful message being delivered, and I think you should think twice before you piggyback on it and to a certain extent disturb it.

In other words, the message that is coming from the Reagan administration in its South African policy is: "Let the market be the prophet." Let it tell the people what is good and what is evil.

It does not take much reflection on the market system for us to recognize that the market is not a divine force. It is not a divine prophet. The invisible hand that Adam Smith made famous, the invisible hand operating behind the scenes, is the hand of IBM and General Motors and the other powerful corporations and people in the system that make the decisions. What Secretary Shultz is saying in effect, then, is "Let the people from the major transnational corporations tell the people who control apartheid to stop. Leave it in their hands. They are, after all, the prophets of truth."

That position echoes one voiced in the early part of this century by Andrew Carnegie in his essay "The Gospel of Wealth." It is part of a tradition rooted in Puritanism that the people who are successful in the pursuit of wealth are obviously God's chosen ones.

This implies that, for the Reagan administration, the people of the U.S. as a nation are not the Chosen People. The Chosen People are the successful business entrepreneurs around the world, the major leaders, the holders of wealth and power. We are supposed to recognize, as Andrew Carnegie preached, that they have been given, as their divine calling, control over the resources of the earth so that they will steward it well on behalf of the people. In that spirit of stewardship, they use some of it to build public service institutions. Divinely selected as the best qualified, they retain control over the resources. In turn, they are expected to assume, in a paternal way, their humanitarian philanthropic responsibilities.

That seems to me to be the underlying spirit of the Reagan administration's position: Just let the economic elite make the decisions and do the prophecy, and it will turn out well for everyone. President Reagan himself sounded that theme when talking about apartheid in July 1986:

> Our own experience teaches us that racial progress comes swiftest and easiest not during economic depression, but in time of prosperity and growth. Our history teaches us that capitalism is the natural enemy of such feudal institutions as apartheid.

He rewrites history extraordinarily! He seems to forget that our system of capitalism has been built upon the suppression of the native population of this land, the destruction of its life and culture. It has been built upon slavery. We had to fight a bloody civil war to eliminate slavery at least as official national policy. He seems to forget the struggle that women had to wage for decades for the simple right to vote and the struggle that still goes on for equality. He seems to forget the Civil Rights movement and ignore the blatant recurrence of racism in recent years. He seems to forget what is happening to our communities all around the country as plants close down and pull out without any concern for the impact on the people. It seems to me that the U.S. Catholic bishops are much closer to the truth and to real prophecy when they suggest in their economic pastoral that any steps toward justice have come as a result of a struggle against the natural workings of the marketplace.

U.S. government policy during this administration has consistently reflected the theology of the gospel of wealth, the theology of the chosenness of the elect few powerful business people. Over these last six years, we have watched the administration take the guts out of our civil rights legislation and undermine its enforcement. We have watched the gap between the wealthy and the poor grow and grow and grow. We have watched the administration build up the military, arming and training it so that it can go anywhere that might be necessary to suppress the rising of the poor and oppressed. We see that in Central America.

We can see this theology at work when we reflect on the amount of money that goes into military production. Military production is high-technology, capital-intensive production. It provides jobs for the people that are best educated, the people whose parents have been able to send them to the best schools. It provides jobs and a secure future for them — and it provides the weapons that will protect their wealth and their lifestyle. One of the real, authentic prophets in my tradition, Archbishop Raymond Hunthausen of Seattle, Washington, has said it very clearly: It is obvious why all these weapons are being built. They are being built to protect our lifestyle from the poor of the world who are rising up and crying out.

Our government's policy, based on this theology of wealth, is creating in our nation and around the world what is increasingly being called "Economic Apartheid." Who are the poor of the world? They are predominantly and disproportionately blacks, Hispanics, people of color everywhere, women, children.

If we use the criterion of "ministry" or "service" to evaluate the record of our government, we can unmask it very easily (see above pp. 56–58). It is a ministry that serves the wealthy as God's Chosen. It hears the cry of the poor and warns that they may be tainted with sinfulness, with Marxism, with the Evil Empire. And it responds to people's yearning for truth with misinformation, public relations, and "great communications."

"The truth will set us free." That is the message of the gospel of Jesus. When we look at the State Theology that is governing our current administration in the U.S., that is not its message. It is not the truth that the administration is presenting us in the name of "freedom." The truth is that we are one with our sisters and brothers in South Africa in their oppression, one with the poor of our nation, one with the poor around the world. They are our family. It is only in our solidarity with them in the struggle against these forces that we have any hope of redemption in fidelity to the Word of God.

Karen Bloomquist

*"The State ... makes use again and again
of the name of God ... "*

— KAIROS DOCUMENT, 2.4

The theology of chosen peoplehood that underlies the South African government's explicit theology is not dissimilar from much of the more covert, secularized U.S. "State Theology" operative in our country today. We need to make U.S. State Theology more explicit.

Not only do we need to point to the similar theological rationalization of state power, but also we need to evaluate critically how these theological symbols function in upholding what *The Nation* called "a global system of political alliances and economic interests that are centered in Washington with South Africa as an outpost of those interests."

From this perspective, South Africa's system and even their State Theology are not separable from our own. To take seriously the critique of State Theology in the Kairos Document necessarily points us to the need for a critique of the State Theology operative here in the U.S., which also contributes toward the rationalization of the continuing system of apartheid in South Africa. Similar code words, such as "communism" and "terrorism," fuel our national policy and seduce us into support of the status quo in South Africa.

We can claim that our critique arises not out of partisan politics but out of a theological understanding of the proper role of the State. But to do that critique necessarily involves moving from

*Karen Bloomquist is Assistant Professor of Church and Society at the Lutheran
School of Theology, Chicago*

abstractions to concrete issues and policies and ideologies and will inevitably be perceived as partisan. It is the particular acts and utterances of our president, congress, and judiciary that reveal how our government fails in its proper and necessary mandate. It fails by equating "law and order" with morality, or by acting primarily to protect vested interest, or by shaping policies and positions primarily out of an absolute fear of the enemy. Perhaps the most telling example of how U.S. State Theology functions is evident in the rhetoric used to justify the so-called Strategic Defense Initiative, which seduces us into believing that we might somehow become invulnerable to attack from our enemies, and especially from our "godless enemy," the USSR.

We need to be clear and specific in naming how the interests of our State are justified:

- What in U.S. State Theology are the primary symbols of evil? Certainly these are centered in the USSR, plus our close neighbor Cuba. But how else is evil symbolized in our national ideologies. How do we become preoccupied with ascertaining who is "atheistic"?

- What encourages us to accept domination and exploitation and how is that related to similar patterns that occur in South Africa?

- How does our State itself become idolatrous? Although it is the government's failure to do the work of justice that is the main criterion for indictment, we cannot de-emphasize the idolatry issue at stake here, lest we miss the radical critique inherent in the Kairos Document for our own situation as a nation.

Our national idolatry and blasphemy may not be as apparent as that embedded in the apartheid constitution. But there are powerful ways in which the myths and ideologies permeating our identity as Americans become an absolute, readily channeled into unquestioned support for a given set of national priorities and policies. We often find ourselves having to choose one set of policies as more adequately serving justice than another set of policies. However, we often fail to go deeper and question whether our popular notions of justice in American society themselves are adequate. They are typically based on ideologies that are individualistic and privatistic and thus "containable" within the operating premises of U.S. capitalism. Motivation based on "me" and "mine" at the cost of the other is, from a biblical perspective, inadequate and moves us into insidiously idolatrous directions. We need to move beyond a critique of which partisan political position would better serve our interest and to ask fundamental questions about "the American dream" and all the ideological underpinnings that fuel our yearnings and our strivings as a nation. We need to ask to what degree some basic issues of idolatry are embedded there.

We need to move into a deeper structural analysis than that typically associated with the Civil Rights movement in this country. We need to be engaged in a deeper socioeconomic analysis in order to take seriously the profound kind of challenges that the Kairos Document presents for our own forms of State Theology.

6

John M. Buchanan

"State Theology is simply the theological justification
of the status quo..."

— KAIROS DOCUMENT, Chap. Two

I'm the pastor of a church not known in Chicago as a hotbed of liberation theology. As I consider the Kairos Document I find myself reminiscing about the fifties and sixties and the beginning of the Civil Rights movement, and how we had to learn not to tell people who felt oppressed that it wasn't appropriate for them to feel oppressed. I recall that we had to learn it again, in regard to another liberation movement — feminism. We had to learn again that it is terribly arrogant to tell someone who is oppressed not to feel oppressed, simply because we don't mean to be oppressors. And so my first response to the Kairos Document is one of modesty and silence. It seems to me that many of us need, first of all, to be humble and to be quiet and to listen very carefully, and to try to identify with the pain and the struggle that is expressed so eloquently in the Kairos Document.

I appreciate the way the document identifies the concept of State Theology. Those of us who live in American middle-class culture must spend a long and humble period of silence before that concept and in dialogue with those who live with its reality. It is important to understand that State Theology is an expression of a dynamic that is always present with the "principalities and powers" from Hezekiah to Caesar to Hitler, and that it is the nature of a State that is unfettered by unaccountability to its people to supplant God. I appreciate the document's simple but eloquent

John M. Buchanan is pastor of the Fourth Presbyterian Church in Chicago.

assertion that this particular State is built on a premise that it is
a good thing to do bad things.

On the other hand I should like to challenge the way the document lists racism, capitalism, and totalitarianism in the same
sentence as if they constitute an inevitable progression. I was dis-
appointed in this oversimplification, particularly in light of the document's own argument that dissent is not automatically socialist-
communist. I propose that you don't have to list racism, capitalism, and totalitarianism as if one always leads to the other, and I
don't think that it follows that people who believe capitalism is a
viable economic system are, ipso facto, racists and totalitarians.

Somehow I made it on the list of religious leaders who were
invited to the recent State Department briefing on South Africa.
And I came home from Washington thinking that perhaps those
of us who dare to stand in pulpits on Sunday mornings have one
simple mission, and that is to tell the truth. We are called to
truth-telling, which sometimes means to resist intellectually the
enormous lying that is going on in regard to South Africa. It's
a time when a religiosity totally divorced from the biblical sense
of peace and justice is very popular and successful, but being an
optimist essentially, I believe truth-telling prevails, and that pur-
veyors of a religion that ignores injustice will ultimately fail. In
fact, signs that the failure has begun are very promising.

With regard to Romans 13, it's about time we began to exegete
over and over again that grossly misused passage. It is helpful to
be reminded so strongly that within Christian history opposition
to an unjust regime is not marginal, fringe activity. It is traditional and mainstream. It is helpful to remember that when we
discuss the public opposition to unjust political powers, we can
invoke some names that are very dear to us. I think it was Robert
McAfee Brown who quoted Abraham Heschel to the effect that if
you listened to the way Romans 13 usually gets interpreted you'd
still be building pyramids in Egypt.

It is good to be reminded that there is a wistful, lovely biblical
tradition about a State that nurtures and feeds. And it seems to
me that this image is particularly compelling as we read the great
Isaiah texts.

Finally, I raise the issue that haunts many of us who find racism
abhorrent, who regard disobedience to an unjust regime as an act
of faith, who nevertheless go to sleep every night wondering how

apartheid can be brought down and a democratic government installed in South Africa without a holocaust. The question is raised by James Armstrong's *Planning for Life After Apartheid*. Perhaps it's my mission to worry about that, and to weep about it and to agonize about it, but not to insist that brothers and sisters in South Africa — whose daily lives are lived out under apartheid — worry about that part. Maybe that's what American middle-class Christians have to do: to weep and worry and trust God's liberating Spirit.

7

Bible Study
by Thomas Hoyt, Jr.

"Every text must be interpreted in its context..."
— KAIROS DOCUMENT, 2.1

¹ Let every person be subject to the governing authorities. For there is no authority except from God, and those that exist have been instituted by God.

² Therefore he who resists the authorities resists what God has appointed, and those who resist will incur judgment.

³ For rulers are not a terror to good conduct, but to bad. Would you have no fear of him who is in authority? Then do what is good and you will receive his approval,

⁴ for he is God's servant for your good. But if you do wrong, be afraid, for he does not bear the sword in vain; he is the servant of God to execute his wrath on the wrongdoer.

⁵ Therefore one must be subject, not only to avoid God's wrath but also for the sake of conscience.

⁶ For the same reason you also pay taxes, for the authorities are ministers of God, attending to this very thing.

⁷ Pay all of them their dues, taxes to whom taxes are due, revenue to whom revenue is due, respect to whom respect is due, honor to whom honor is due.

[Romans 13:1–7 RSV]

The authors of the Kairos Document encourage us to enter into dialogue with them. Recognizing that this document is the product

Thomas Hoyt, Jr., is Professor of New Testament and Director of the Black Ministries Certificate Program at Hartford Seminary Foundation, Hartford, Conn.

of the experiences of oppressed people who are informed by biblical interpretations, my dialogical point of entry will be biblical analysis. Here we shall consider Romans 13:1–7, a text frequently quoted in the document, and test one of the conclusions of the document, namely, that this text is not meant as a biblical sanction for obedience to every State, regardless of the manner in which that State governs.

It is important to deal with Romans 13 because it has been used by "State Theology" to provide theological justification for the status quo: racism, capitalism, and totalitarianism. Consequently injustice is blessed and the will of the powerful dominates those who are poor and tyrannizes them into obedience or passivity. All of this is done in the name of a biblical mandate.

Romans 13:1–7 does not intend to present a full outline of Paul's view of government, and even less a "doctrine of the State." (Unfortunately, the Jerusalem Bible translates v. 4 as "the state is there to serve God for your benefit"; there is no word for "State" in the text.) We should also remember that Paul did not address the question of whether civil disobedience is ever called for by a Christian living under a corrupt, unjust, racist government. He was not attempting to write a manifesto for the church's relationship to governments for all centuries. His concern was local and specific. Nevertheless, he was affirming that a proper understanding of, and lifestyle in relation to, the State is part of one's "spiritual worship" (12:1–2). Religion and politics do meet — at least in the Bible.

Paul's formulae for the mixture might be summarized as follows: (1) desire for peace, justice, and order in accordance with God's purpose for creation, and (2) concern for that which fosters harmony and unity in the church so that the church may carry out its redemptive mission. These concerns (which are grounded in Rom. 13:1–7), rather than a blind, unconditional commitment to any and every civil authority, should guide the Christian's attitude toward the State.

On the surface, Romans 13:1–7 conveys the message that we should obey rulers and pay taxes. What is obvious, however, may be deceptive if we do not examine the contexts of this important text. Let us look first at the historical context.

Historical Context

Romans was written at the end of the 50s — possibly in 56 or
early in 58 — to a community Paul had not founded and which
he had never visited. The church in the Roman capital was a
mixture of Gentile and Jewish Christians practically all of whom
had been deeply influenced by Jerusalem missionaries. While deliberately revising and restating his theological position, Paul is
worried about his strained relationship with leading persons in the
Jerusalem church and the possible objections he might meet in his
fund-raising campaign (Rom. 15:30–31). In Romans, Paul seems
to set forth what he will ultimately say to his fellow Christians in
Jerusalem. But Paul also has to say a word to the Roman Christians with regard to the powers that be.

There is disagreement among the experts on why Paul writes so
positively about the governing authorities; there are several possible explanations.

First, Paul was writing early in Nero's reign, when people were
still optimistic about the potential of Nero's rule. Less than ten
years before the letter to the Romans was written, Claudius had
expelled Jews from the city, including Jewish Christians. Suetonius
contends that "Claudius expelled the Jews from Rome because of
their constant disturbances impelled by Chrestus." By the time
Romans was written, Claudius had died (A.D. 54) and many Jews
had returned to Rome; the general atmosphere cleared up and
Rome entered a period of relatively good government. Nero, who
followed Claudius, was at first extremely popular. The empire was
virtually under the control of Seneca. Nero was only nineteen or
twenty years of age when Paul wrote this letter, and the atrocities
of Nero's reign had not yet been executed. Perhaps Paul wanted to
avoid giving Nero any excuse to repeat the precedent of Claudius.
Paul may have known how precarious the legal status of the Christian house churches was in Rome and may have wanted to head
off any harassment. It has been suggested that Paul would have
written differently had he foreseen the persecution Nero was to
command.

A second explanation has to do with the nature of salvation.
Paul is dealing with a tendency, assumed to be present in Rome no
less than in his own churches, to regard with contempt the institutions and laws of this world because Christians are "free from the

law" altogether. Variations of this theme may have come from pre-gnostic influences, apocalyptists, and eschatological enthusiasts. Christians who were influenced by pre-gnostic ideas advocated a kind of Christian anarchism as a sign of their complete liberation from this world. Those influenced by an apocalyptic mindset probably asserted that the government and its agents were instruments of Satan. Eschatological enthusiasts felt that the contingent world was irrelevant because the end was near.

This eschatological point of view may help us in understanding Paul's own view of the State. The State in this view is a temporary institution that is willed by God only for the duration of the present age. When Christ comes again there will be no need for the State. It is consistent with Pauline theology to look at the State as a temporary institution that will soon be superseded.

A third explanation for Paul's view of the positive role of governing authorities is his own experience with them in his missionary ventures. Paul often used his Roman citizenship as a badge of honor and protection. Julius Caesar and Augustus had improved and guaranteed the legal status of Jews in the Roman empire. Paul was a beneficiary of that improvement.

Like many in the Roman provinces, Paul was thankful for Roman peace, order, justice, and administration, which made possible his missionary journeys, rescued him from violent mobs, and restrained social evils. Gallio, as governor of Achaia, dismissed charges that the local synagogue brought against Paul in Corinth in A.D. 51. Acts 21:31ff. reports that Paul was rescued from a lynch mob in Jerusalem by the Roman commander of the fortress Antonia. Thus some would hold that Paul spoke favorably of Rome because he wished to dispel the view that Christians were political agitators working against the Roman peace.

Paul's Worldview

In the worldview of Paul's day there existed a strong and significant relationship between civil rulers and spiritual powers. According to a common Greco-Roman concept of the State, the ruler was divinely appointed and was part of a cosmic system of spiritual powers.[1]

This concept of the State was so widely accepted that "where Paul, Hellenistic Jews, or early Christians do not openly oppose it we should first of all assume that it was taken for granted until it is found incompatible in some particular."[2] This information is important for understanding the thought process behind Paul's writing on the State.

Scholars contend that Romans 13:1–7 resembles the passage found in the Wisdom of Solomon 6:1–11 with its allusion to "the Kings of the earth, to whom God has delegated authority." Romans 13:1–7 is also similar to the rabbinical saying that "to resist the King is to pitch oneself against the Skekinah." These background texts help us to understand better Paul's view of the relation between Christians' actions and the authorities.

Christians are to perform good deeds in order to win the approval of authorities. "Would you have no fear of him who is in authority? Then do what is good and you will receive his approval" (v. 3). Just as "judgment" in verse 2 is God's judgment, so also is the powers' commendation a divine commendation (v. 3). The authorities in Roman society usually bestowed commendation upon those who made outstanding contributions to the welfare of the State by erecting statues of them and having public inscriptions made to them.

Do the authorities, literally "powers," refer to earthly rulers, to demonic powers, or to angels? We know that in the ancient world "secular reality" was not just secular. Politics and cosmology were intricately related. In fact, the degree to which angelic powers influenced political rulers in the worldview of Judaism and Paul has been discussed by many scholars. Fitzmyer's practical approach will suffice for our purpose: "What is primary in Paul's affirmation is the relation of the Christian to the secular government, whether this be regarded as entirely human or as controlled by angelic spirits."[3]

Verse 1, the general statement (v. 1a) and its reason (v. 1b), underscores that those who are in power, even the officials with whom the ordinary Christian comes into contact, belong to the divine order. This is brought home forcefully: twice we hear the expression "by God"; the verb "have been instituted" is in the perfect tense, i.e., it denotes an action completed in the past, but whose effects are regarded as continuing in the present. (The "every person" in v. 1 means every Christian, not every inhabitant of the empire; Paul's letters never address the public at large.)

Literary Context

When Romans 13:1–7 is interpreted in the light of the surrounding text, we note two points that help us understand Paul's attitude toward the State. First, the matter under discussion at this point is the Christian commandment of love: evil is not to be rewarded with evil; rather we are to do good to our enemies. This stands in 12:17–21 immediately before the section on the State in Romans 13:1–7; directly afterwards, in Romans 13:8, the same theme is resumed. Second, the expectation of the End is also under discussion: the night is far spent, the day draws near (Rom. 13:11–14).[4]

Romans 13:1–7 has literary affinities with the advice current in Hellenistic Judaism concerning respect for the State and its rulers. Paul would seem to be instructing the Roman churches, especially the Jewish churches in Rome, to keep to the tradition that had formed their political posture. Paul's advice is compatible with the wisdom of Hellenistic Judaism when he argues that rulers are appointed by God (13:1–2), that their legitimate function is to protect the innocent, promote the good, and punish the evil (13:3–4), and that those who desire a well- ordered community life ought to render the authorities appropriate taxes and honor (13:5–7). Paul offers that advice, that moral wisdom, in a new context, a transforming context. It is part of his call for a new discernment (Rom. 12:1–2), and he sets before it and behind it reminders of the eschatological situation (12:2; 13:11–12) and of the duty to love (12:9; 13:8). Submission to government is set in the context of the more urgent duty to love our neighbor while we await God's justice.

Conditional Obedience

Two reasons for obedience to authorities are introduced: divine punishment and conscience. Paul contends that we must insert ourselves in God's order "not only to avoid God's wrath but also for the sake of conscience" (v. 5).

Authorities use force to punish wrong in the name of God. Verse 3 contends that "rulers are not a terror to good conduct, but to bad." In general, in Hebrew scriptures "terror" is attributed to God, not powers. Here, however, rulers are a terror, because they are agents of divine wrath: "he is the servant of God to execute his wrath on the wrongdoer" (v. 4). The State represents God's abhorrence of evil. God's wrath, which belongs properly to the last day (Rom. 2:5), can be brought forward into the present (Rom. 1:18). By God's will even the fallen world can point to manifestations and instruments of the order that God has established.

In verse 4 we are told that the ruler "is God's servant for your good." The politician, the ruler of the people, is called God's servant. Here for the first time in our unit we sense a shift in focus. Power implies both authority and responsibility; political institutions imply both gift and task. Government shares in the coveted God-given drive toward order. But in the same breath Paul affirms that the "good" is a *task* entrusted to civil authority. The good is not automatic. So, embedded in v. 4a lies a fundamental limitation of all human authority. The text implicitly says that the ruler who loses sight of the function of serving the good loses his or her authority.

If the ruler is truly the servant of God, then that ruler must keep within the bounds of God's will. According to master-slave logic, if a servant does not follow the master's will then the other servants are not supposed to follow the disobedient servant. Implicit, therefore, in Paul's imagery is a conditional obedience.

Verse 6 shows another example of the Christians' insertion in God's order: "For the same reason you also pay taxes." In calling tax collectors "ministers of God," Paul remains consistent with what he said in v. 4. He again stresses the delegated character of civil authorities. (But Paul's idea is difficult to accept if we remember that in the Hellenistic world only 20 percent of the collected taxes reached Rome while 80 percent remained in the hands of the greedy intermediaries.)

Through the passage, Paul quietly sets government authority under the authority of God. There is no blurring of lines between political power and divine power. The real power to be respected ultimately is God's. Government has God-given responsibility for the good (v. 4: literally, "God's servant for you for the good").

"Respect" and "honor" in verse 7 probably relate to the authorities (v. 3). Since "respect" is uniquely related to God, some interpreters would detect here an echo of the gospel saying: "Render to Caesar the things that are Caesar's and to God the things that are God's" (Mark 12:17). In this case we would touch in v. 7b still another limitation to obedience.

In any case, Paul does not write what the emperors would have preferred him to write: that the emperor embodies a divine genius or power. Likewise, when Paul asks that honor be given to whomever honor is due, he does not say that this includes divine honor.

Another factor conditioning obedience to the governing authorities concerns Paul's understanding of conscience. This Hellenistic word has several meanings. It certainly has to do with a person's awareness of what is right. Originally, it meant the pain one feels when one does something wrong. Paul deepens this into an assessing discernment amid "conflicting thoughts," an evaluating capacity that operates as a criterion for right or wrong because of the coming judgment (Rom. 2:14–15). It is the reflecting and judging "I" of faith that seeks to determine in various situations what the will of God is. If Paul appeals to such a conscience in the matter of obedience to authority, then he opens the door for conscientious disobedience or selective obedience.

When Romans 13:1–7 is read in its literary and historical context, we see that Paul does not require uncritical obedience to the State regardless of how unjust or pernicious the regime. We conclude with the authors of the Kairos Document: " 'The State is there to serve God for your benefit,' says Paul. That is the kind of State he is speaking of. That is the kind of State that must be obeyed. In this text Paul does not tell us what we should do when a State does *not* serve God and does *not* work for the benefit of all but has become unjust and oppressive. That is another question" (Kairos Document, 2.2).

Notes

1. Clinton D. Morrison, *The Powers That Be: Earthly Rulers and Demonic Powers in Rom. 13:1–7* (London: SCM Press, 1960), p. 99.

2. Ibid.

3. R. Brown, J. Fitzmyer, R. Murphy, in *Jerome Biblical Commentary*, section 53:123 (Englewood Cliffs, N.J.: Prentice-Hall, 1968), p. 326.

4. Oscar Cullmann, *The State in the New Testament* (New York: Scribner's, 1956), p. 56.

Part Three
CHURCH THEOLOGY

8

Sheila Briggs

*"Both oppressor and oppressed
claim a loyalty to the same church..."*

—KAIROS DOCUMENT, Chap. One

Alfred Loisy, the Catholic theologian and biblical scholar, made the famous remark at the beginning of this century that Jesus preached the kingdom of God but the church came. This statement expresses Loisy's doubts and also the doubts of the authors of the Kairos Document as to whether their particular church really is in continuity with the message of Jesus of Nazareth. Loisy's aphorism also implies one of the presuppositions that is fundamental to the Kairos Document, namely, that the church is an implication of the praxis of Jesus' followers. Jesus did not found a church, as Loisy was eager to point out. Jesus' praxis of preaching the reign of God and embodying it in his own actions on behalf of the poor, the oppressed, and the suffering, called for an imitation in the praxis of his followers. After Jesus' death and the experience of his resurrection Jesus' followers gathered to form a community to continue his praxis. The church was the result. Ecclesiology, the doctrine of the church, is therefore always secondary to and the corollary of a Christian understanding of praxis.

I have used the word "praxis" to describe the actions of Jesus of Nazareth and how they were imitated in the deeds of his followers. The word "praxis" has been borrowed by liberation theologies from the Marxist tradition and socialist political organizations. It thus has a progressive ring to it. However, Marx himself borrowed it

Sheila Briggs is Assistant Professor, School of Religion, University of Southern California.

from the wider philosophical tradition that goes back ultimately to Aristotle. In Aristotelian philosophy praxis was conceived as the deliberate and voluntary exercise of virtue; and virtue was understood as the excellence of a person for action most fitted to his or her nature.

Marx did not claim that socialism was the only form of praxis and that other political theories were simply philosophical abstractions. Instead, he was aware of the inevitability of praxis. All ideologies, all systems of ideas, all worldviews, are inextricably linked to a certain social praxis, however abstract their formulations may be. All ideas are practiced. Thus, praxis, or simply practice, is basic to the life of any group or institution. Marx revised the Aristotelian concept of virtue, seeing praxis not as the attempt to conform one's action to virtue, to the nature and goal of one's existence, but rather asserting that virtue conforms to praxis. Our life is not directed by any goals intrinsic to our nature but by the goals that emerge from our social practices and then become constitutive of our existence.

A Community of Practice

To ask about the "nature" of the church requires that we ask about the social practice by virtue of which the church is the church. The church is a community of practice; it cannot avoid being a community of practice. The crucial question becomes what is its praxis. Is the praxis of the Christian church in continuity with and an authentic imitation of the praxis of Jesus of Nazareth? In its critique of Church Theology the Kairos Document gives the answer that the praxis of the churches in South Africa contradicts the gospel practiced in the life of Jesus of Nazareth. The Kairos Document urges the recognition of the fact that "the church is divided against itself and its day of judgment has come." It is divided by the conflict of social practices within it. In resolving this division appeal cannot be made to the "nature" of the church. The church does not have another nature than that of being the community of a particular practice. There is no apolitical perspective on the role of the church in its social reality. The Kairos Document correctly diagnoses the fundamental problem of Church Theology as related to its lack of social analysis and its lack of an adequate understanding of politics and political strategy. These deficiencies amount to having no ecclesiology, i.e., a clear discernment of the nature of the church in South Africa.

I am somewhat hesitant to share the view of the Kairos Document that the fundamental problem of Church Theology and the reason for its lack of social analysis and an adequate understanding of politics and political strategy lie in the "type of faith and spirituality that has dominated church life for centuries. As we all know, spirituality has tended to be an otherworldly affair that has very little, if anything at all, to do with the affairs of this world" (3.4). Instead, I would argue that Church Theology is in the full Aristotelian sense a deliberate and voluntary exercise of the virtue of the church in South Africa, i.e., the intrinsic aims of its existence as defined by its leaders.

As a historian of theology I know of no epoch in the church's history when the encouragement of Christians to set their sights upon heaven has not entailed specific prescriptions about how to live their life upon earth. Only since the eighteenth century have the Christian churches been excluded from the exercise of political power and given up their claim to such. This adjustment to secularization in the modern period has been slow and in some cases incomplete, such as in the Roman Catholic church. Even in the churches where secularization has been most thorough it has not encompassed a total renunciation of social power by the Christian churches. Instead, the churches have agreed not to encroach on the power of the State in exchange for a position of social prestige, for tangible social privileges, and for a limited but nonetheless real role in some areas of social policy — a point to which I will return later.

Church Theology is situated in the leadership of the "English-speaking" churches of South Africa, which are akin to the liberal Protestant churches of Europe and North America and which have actively sought a compromise with the State similar to their Northern counterparts. The South African State has the trappings of the Western liberal democracies but is, in fact, closer to the national security states of the Latin American dictatorships. José Comblin has described the temptation that the national security State in Latin America has presented the churches there by offering them social recognition and privilege in exchange for becoming instruments of the State's ideology and social policy.[1] In most cases the churches in Latin America have resisted this temptation. The churches of Church Theology in South Africa have made this pact with the State. They have as much disingenuously as uncritically adopted the anti-communism of the State ideology as their own, knowing full well that it was directed against the liberation movements of the African people. What the Kairos Document rightly disparages as an "ambulance ministry" (5.2) has been undertaken as a conscious alternative to a social pastorate that conscientizes the people to their oppression and to their resources to bring about change. Church Theology is a praxis, a deliberate and voluntary exercise of the virtue by which the church is not the community of practice that imitates the praxis of Jesus of Nazareth.

Church Theology avoids social analysis and an investigation of politics and political strategy for fear that the nature of its church be revealed as not the community of practice that imitates the praxis of Jesus of Nazareth. In doing so it shows itself not so much as being otherworldly but as thoroughly this-worldly. Its apolitical stance, its neutrality are predicated upon its commitment to the world as it is at present. Church Theology is a political epistemology, by which I mean that it seeks to know human beings and human society in a way that is consistent with a particular organization of the State and society. It submits itself to a form of cognitive self-limitation, seeing only the possibilities for South Africans and their society that the apartheid system presents. Church Theology claims to "know" that the alternatives facing South Africa are cautious and gradual reform or subversion and revolution. On the basis of this "knowledge" it asserts that the only rational and humane solution to South Africa's problems is to choose the course of cautious and gradual reform. Its vision is restricted to the social construction of reality by the institutions of apartheid.

In response to the position of Church Theology snugly ensconced within the present social reality one needs to remember the critique of "the world" found in the New Testament, especially the Johannine writings. The epistemological blindness of the world is revealed in that it does not know Jesus and the one who sent him (John 14:17). When the Holy Spirit comes, we are told, it will force the conviction upon the world as to what really is sin, justice, and judgment. The world will be compelled to recognize that it is under judgment because the "ruler of the world" has been cast down (John 16:8–11). The present social reality of injustice is condemned; so are the political and economic, the social and cultural forces, and the religious forces that govern it. The distinction that Afro-American Christianity has made between the sacred and profane says much the same thing. This differentiation is not equivalent to one between the church and secular society but rather attests the sharp opposition between the sphere in which justice reigns and the other sphere in which injustice dominates.

The arguments of Church Theology at first glance seem plausible because they are framed within the cognitive structures of the present reality. For example, the call for reconciliation and negotiation seems to be the most effective way of reaching political solutions and social agreements. But such apparent reasonableness is based on a false perception of reality, one that serves the preservation of the status quo. The Kairos Document points out that the conflict in South Africa is not the result of "misunderstandings" between two groups of people. Clarification and compromise are illusory means for bringing about the end of this confrontation because two opposing realities are facing one another. There is the reality of the present world of apartheid and the reality of that other world in which the oppressed are liberated. The Kairos Document portrays this clash in terms as drastic as any to be found in the Gospel of John or elsewhere in the New Testament. "There are conflicts that can only be described as the struggle between justice and injustice, good and evil, God and the devil" (3.1).

A Divided Community

The church in South Africa is divided today because there are diverse and opposing communities of practice within it. Is there any element, any heritage common to all Christian churches in South Africa that could unite them? Recently some theologians have suggested that the Christian community gathers to tell a story. If the diverse practice of Christians divides the church, can a common story unite it? The problem with a narrative reconstruction of the Christian community and its social ethics is that it rests on the assumption that Christians share the same story or stories. Stanley Hauerwas has argued the unity of Christians is guaranteed against the dividedness of the world through the stories of Israel and Jesus. When faced with the objection that Christians are just as fragmented in their moral stances as other groups in society, Hauerwas replies that he is not describing Christians as they are but Christians as they should be. Interestingly, Hauerwas also wants to return to a virtue-conception of morality, seeing virtue as the unity of the moral life. Yet he sees the virtues as insufficient in themselves to restore the moral unity of the individual and communal self if these are not themselves grounded in story.[2]

But what is the relationship of praxis to story? It is reasonably accurate to claim that in accounts that view the church as a community constituted through a common narrative, praxis becomes seen as the implication of story. The church is not the church because it does justice, but because it tells the story of the just God. Certainly, telling the story of the just God should issue in a praxis of justice. But the incompleteness with which the church engages in a praxis of justice does not undermine its existence as church; rather it makes the church inconsistent with its own self. The virtue through which the church is the church, in this view, is grounded primarily in story and only secondarily realized in praxis.

Against this priority given to story as the foundational and unifying constituent of the church I contend that Christians belong to communities of divided stories because they belong to communities of divided practices. It is not simply the case that in different contexts, in different historical and cultural situations Christians tell different stories. It is a fact — and a fact in South Africa today — that Christians in the same context tell opposing stories. In such a situation one can maintain that Christians should be telling the same story or stories, but the reason why they are telling opposing stories is because they are involved in opposing practices. A narrative recounts what fictional characters or real people do. A narrative undoubtedly discloses the self of the persons whose actions it portrays but it does this through delineating the relationship of the self to the actions described. Stories are about praxis. Communities of story are identical with communities of practice, not transcendent of them.

The Hermeneutical Question

It is not enough to say that all Christian communities narrate the biblical story, the stories of Israel and of Jesus. On the formal level, Christians may indeed tell the same story or set of stories, but the meaning of these stories is disclosed in Christian praxis. In South Africa today what the biblical stories are about depends on who

you are and what you do, whether you are among the oppressed or
the oppressors. In the Kairos Document as in other Third World
theologies of liberation the Exodus story is invoked as paradigmatic
of the way in which God sides with the oppressed. God's justice is
implemented through the struggle of the oppressed for liberation
and is not something of which the oppressor is capable. "God will
bring about change," the Kairos Document says, "through the oppressed as he did through the oppressed Hebrew slaves in Egypt.
God does not bring his justice through reforms introduced by the
Pharaohs of this world" (3.2). In South Africa it is not only the
African people struggling for their liberation who take the Exodus
story as a model of God's justice for the oppressed. The white
Afrikaners have developed since the nineteenth century an elaborate theology of domination in which the Exodus story is also
central. In the politico-religious ritual of the Day of Covenant,
Afrikaners commemorate the massacre of Africans at the Battle
of Blood River during the Great Trek of the last century. In this
retelling of the Exodus story the Afrikaners are the people of Israel, the Great Trek is the Exodus journey to freedom, the land
of South Africa is the land given to them as the chosen people by
God, and the Africans are the peoples of Canaan to be given over
to slaughter and reduced to slavery.[3]

One can argue that the Afrikaner theology of domination and
genocide is a distortion of the Exodus story. Historical study of
the Bible does suggest that the Hebrews belonged to the disinherited of the land of Canaan and kindred groups in the surrounding
countries, and therefore it would be wrong to equate the Exodus
with a foreign invasion in the way that the Pharaoh of Egypt might
have invaded the King of Assyria.[4] The experience of the ancient
Hebrews is closer to that of black South Africans than it is to
that of white Afrikaners. Yet on the formal level white Afrikaners
are interpreting the Exodus story in the same way as the Kairos
Document, i.e., they are relating the biblical story to present experience. The white Afrikaners would assert that they too were
oppressed and disinherited (by the coming of British rule to South
Africa). In the end it is not appeal to historical evidence that
can decide which experience — that of the black South African or
the white Afrikaner — is the authentic context in which the Exodus story can be retold. If whatever God's justice is belongs to a
remote and obscure past, then it is irrelevant to anybody's experi-

ence. God's justice lives. It lives in present experience but not in all present experience. God's justice and liberation are promised not to those who can allege a formal similarity between their experience and the experience of the oppressed people of Israel in the ancient Near East but to those who within the context of today's society can rightfully claim to be the oppressed.

In the background of the Kairos Document there is a biblical hermeneutic. The document in several places refers to its task as presenting a biblical reflection on the crisis in South Africa. In the preface the process by which the Kairos Document came into existence is elucidated. Anyone and everyone could contribute to it as long as his or her position could "stand the test of biblical faith and Christian experience in South Africa." The juxtaposition of biblical faith and Christian experience in South Africa underlines the need to interpret the Bible in the light of present experience. But it is clear from the whole tenor of the Kairos Document that the experience of the oppressor — the white minority in South Africa — cannot be used to judge the truthfulness of the Kairos Document's witness to what God's demands for justice in the present-day situation of South Africa are.

Church Theology is unbiblical because it attempts to find biblical faith in the Christianity of communities that practice oppression. Church Theology is unbiblical in this way not because it does not know the biblical texts but because it does not know the Spirit that speaks through them. Church Theology looks at the Bible as a supposedly well-balanced repository of spiritual encouragement for all, words of comfort and hope not only for the oppressed but also for the oppressor. It can quote numerous passages from the Bible that present the perspective of the oppressor, the concern for good social order through a hierarchy in which some hold power over others. It cannot be denied that there are biblical texts that uphold the authority of the slaveholder rather than preach liberation to the slaves. In the household code of Ephesians 5:22–6:9 wives are urged to submit to their husbands and slaves to obey their masters "with fear and trembling." It is impossible to reconcile the Ephesians household code with Galatians 3:28, which proclaims there is no longer Jew nor Greek, slave nor free, male nor female, but all are one in Christ Jesus. But this is precisely the approach of Church Theology in that it demands of Christians in South Africa that they "listen to both sides of the story" (3.1).

The biblical texts represent several communities of practice that adopted different narrative strategies toward the stories of Israel and Jesus where their social practices disagreed.

How do we discern the authentic biblical message in the biblical texts? The Christian tradition has made the distinction between the spirit and the letter, the Holy Spirit who speaks through the biblical texts and the surface meaning of the biblical texts that may contradict one another and the inspiration of the Holy Spirit. In the Afro-American religious experience the slaves distinguished between the "massa's Bible," from which their owners read constantly exhortations to slaves to obey their masters, and the real Bible that knew of no justification of slavery. American slaveholders exploited the fact that most of their slaves could not read the Bible — teaching a slave to read and write was a criminal offense. The slaves responded that the oppressor could never have power over the Bible, could never own its meaning. In South Africa today, the Kairos Document is repeating the claim of the Afro-American slaves. Behind the profession of the Kairos Document that its statements rest on biblical faith is the conviction that it is the oppressed who hear what the Spirit is saying through the Bible. The oppressors may read many things in Scripture that comfort them but they will never hear the Spirit, because the Spirit speaks only in the experience of the oppressed.

This is the hermeneutical privilege of the oppressed. Church Theology tries to take this privileged understanding of the biblical message away from the oppressed. It pretends that the Spirit is speaking where the Spirit is not speaking: in the experience of the oppressor. The Spirit speaks in the experience of the oppressors only at that point when they realize they are such, when they become aware of their need for repentance and forgiveness and that repentance and forgiveness can be obtained only through ceasing to do injustice and beginning to do justice. The Kairos Document issues this warning to those who would let themselves be comforted as oppressors by Church Theology: "The biblical teaching on reconciliation and forgiveness makes it quite clear that nobody can be forgiven and reconciled with God unless he or she repents of their sins.... Reconciliation, forgiveness, and negotiations will become our Christian duty only when the apartheid regime shows signs of genuine repentance" (3.1). To know a Bible that preaches reconciliation, forgiveness, and negotiations now in South Africa, as

Church Theology asserts, is not to know the Bible through which
the Spirit speaks; in the words of the apostle Paul to the Christian
community in Galatia, it is to preach a gospel other than that of
Jesus Christ.

Critique from the Underside

Having discarded the false biblical hermeneutic of Church Theology the way is open for the Kairos Document to develop an authentic understanding of the Christian themes of reconciliation, justice,
and non-violence within the context of South Africa today. Reading the Kairos Document's treatment of reconciliation, justice, and
non-violence I was struck by its similarity to the final chapter of
James Cone's book *Black Theology and Black Power*. Published
in 1969, Cone's book expressed the righteous anger of black Americans against white Americans at the close of the Civil Rights era
when they saw that white America was trying to ameliorate racial
oppression by reforms that would cement its own hold on power
instead of attacking the deeply embedded structures of racism in
American society that robbed blacks of their socioeconomic well-
being, their cultural flourishing, their mental and physical lives.
The characteristics of racial oppression in South Africa are very
similar to those that Cone described, only they exist in an even
more drastic form.

In the chapter titled "Revolution, Violence and Reconciliation
in Black Theology," Cone writes:

To speak of Satan and his powers becomes not just a way
of speaking but a fact of reality. When we can see a people
who are controlled by an ideology of whiteness, then we know
what reconciliation must mean. The coming of Christ means
a denial of what we thought we were. It means destroying the
white devil in us. Reconciliation to God means that white
people are prepared to deny themselves (whiteness), take up
the cross (blackness) and follow Christ (black Ghetto).[5]

Church Theology rejects the radical reconciliation that a faithful
imitation of the praxis of Jesus requires in the South African situation. The white minority is not urged to transform the comfortable
lifestyle of the white suburbs into the sufferings of blacks in Soweto,

other black townships, and the tribal homelands. The Kairos Document reminds us that "we are supposed to oppose, confront, and reject the devil and not try to sup with the devil" (3.1).

The Kairos Document discusses how justice can come to South Africa. It rejects the "justice of reform" because that is a false kind of justice, a justice that is perceived as being the gift of the oppressor. Church Theology appeals to the oppressor to institute justice because it is not located in the community of the practice among oppressed Christians. As the Kairos Document puts it, "appeals from the 'top' in the church tend very easily to be appeals to the 'top' in society," and the Kairos Document adds: "real change and true justice can only come from below, from the people — most of whom are Christians" (3.2).

What means do the oppressed in a very repressive society have of creating justice? The African National Congress after the brutal suppression of its peaceful agitation for black freedom moved to the position that the liberation of blacks in South Africa should be sought "by any means necessary." This has led to the initiation of armed struggle to topple the apartheid regime. Church Theology has condemned such action and pleaded instead for non-violence as the only way to a political solution in South Africa. The Kairos Document undertakes a critique of Church Theology's call for non-violence. At the core of its critique is a distinction between the physical force that the apartheid regime uses to maintain injustice and the physical force that the oppressed in South Africa use to resist and liberate themselves. The Kairos Document rejects the blanket use of the term "violence" to describe the coercion used by the oppressor to maintain a system of injustice as well as the physical force used to overthrow it by the oppressed. The Kairos Document wishes to reserve the term "violence" for the action of the oppressor. Church Theology condemns the violence committed by the oppressed blacks in South Africa, while at the same time conceding the white minority government the right to use coercion to preserve the social order. An unjust social order is by its very nature violent, and thus one cannot avoid condoning its use of violence if one grants it a right to self-defense.

Although I agree with the basic point the Kairos Document is making here, I cannot help but find its biblical argumentation faulty. The Kairos Document is generally correct in its explanation that "throughout the Bible the word 'violence' is used to describe everything that is done by a wicked oppressor.... It is never used to describe the activities of Israel's armies in attempting to liberate themselves or to resist aggression" (3.3). But then it is universally the case that a negatively loaded word such as "violence" is never used for the physical force that one's own group employs but always for the physical force used by others against one's group. When the Canaanites slew the Israelites it was violence; when the Israelites slew the Canaanites it was God's command. The militaristic patriarchy that governs South Africa today can to some extent rightly claim a forerunner in ancient Israel. The word "violence" in ancient Israel, by which the Kairos Document refers specifically to the Hebrew *ḥāmām/ḥāmās*, belonged to an ideology that saw the use of physical force against one's community by others outside it as by definition unjust. As the Kairos Document concludes, "what one calls 'violence' and what one calls 'self-defense' seems to depend upon which side one is on" (3.3).

For a Beloved Community

The Kairos Document does not romanticize revolutionary violence nor does it advocate the indiscriminate use of violence by the oppressed. However, it does neglect the reasons why Bishop Desmond Tutu, like Martin Luther King, Jr., before him here in the United States, espouses non-violence. I do not believe that the Kairos Document is lumping Bishop Tutu together with Church Theology, any more than the earlier critique of non-violence in American black theology identified Martin Luther King, Jr., with white attempts to contain the black struggle through appeals to non-violence. The non-violence of Martin Luther King, Jr., or Bishop Tutu has the liberation of the oppressed as its highest goal; it recognizes evil as evil and rejects it as such. It also clearly envisages the kind of society that it desires to emerge from the struggle for liberation which is — in Martin Luther King, Jr.'s words — "the beloved community." Violence or physical force, or whatever else one may name it, leaves persons dead, maimed, children orphaned, lives shattered, regardless of who uses it. These are not the conditions under which one can build the "beloved community." Power may grow out of a barrel of a gun but a new humanity does not, and it is a new humanity, not power, that is the ultimate aim of the oppressed, whether they use peaceful or violent means.

On the other side, the Kairos Document reminds us that we cannot apply the standards of moral perfectionism to a situation of oppression. The authors of the Kairos Document, like James Cone earlier, invoke the theology of Bonhoeffer, who participated in a plot to assassinate Hitler and was killed by the Nazis. The oppressed may be required reluctantly to employ physical force as a last resort as "the lesser of two guilts," a phrase the Kairos Document borrows from Bonhoeffer (3.3). James Cone insists that Christian ethics does not presuppose that the believer is in possession of an infallible code as to what is good and evil, but is placed by God under the necessity to act. He quotes once more from Bonhoeffer:

> The knowledge of Jesus is entirely transformed into action, without any reflection upon a man's self. A man's own goodness is now concealed from him. It is not merely that he is no longer obliged to be judge of his own goodness; he must no longer desire to know of it at all, or rather he is no longer permitted to know of it at all.[6]

Christian communities are called to imitate the praxis of Jesus of Nazareth not by being communities of perfect practice. Indeed faithfulness to Jesus may involve them in being to some degree communities of guilty practice.

The conditions for a beloved community are certainly not in any way contained in the present unjust society where the violence of the oppressors already dehumanizes the oppressed struggling for their liberation by violent or by peaceful means because it perceives them as the enemy, as subversives whom one has the right to suppress by any means possible, including the torture and murder of schoolchildren. There is a basic fallacy in the argument, often advanced by those who at present enjoy privilege, that all that happens in a revolution is that the oppressor and the oppressed change places. The self-serving implication is, of course, that one might as well leave things as they are. If through the use of physical force the oppressed do not create the conditions for the "beloved community," they at least open the possibility for the least oppressive society possible.

The least oppressive society possible may not be the final goal of Christian social praxis, but it can be the immediate one, a beginning for working toward an increasingly humane society in South

Africa. South African society needs radical transformation. It is not a society with a single oppression but one where injustice permeates the whole web of social relations. Alongside the horrendous racism in South Africa today, there also exist other oppressions of women and of gays. The authors of the Kairos Document have yet to develop a critique of "Culture Theology." Spirituality in South Africa has not been, as the Kairos Document too simply states, "purely private and individualistic" (3.4) The social construction of gender and sexuality in South Africa has been utilized in a theology of domination to portray white control as the bulwark against African savagery that would rape "unprotected" white women, even the homely matron suckling her child. In reality, the contrary occurs: black women are raped by white employers and policemen, but the pornographic sexist image of the raped white woman feeds the resolve of white men to preserve their brutal racial supremacy.

The ultimate charge that can be levelled against Church Theology is that it has hindered a peaceful and radical transformation of South African society. It has reduced the need for change to an overcoming of an unfortunate stage in race relations rather than the introduction of universal equality (with majority rule), the establishing of universal civil and human rights in a society that fundamentally lacks these. It therefore fails to see the urgency of the situation and that the *kairos* of South African society and its churches has arrived when a decision must be made between justice and destruction.

Yet neither Church Theology nor its disastrous effect on South Africa is limited to the southern tip of Africa. For a quarter of this century the oppressed peoples of South Africa have been appealing to the countries of North America and Europe to wield the enormous power of their economic, political, and military connections with South Africa to bring about change. For most of this long period this cry has been unheeded. The appeal to the "top" of world society had as little result as that to the "top" of South African society. Church Theology in the Western nations issued the same calls for non-violence to the oppressed peoples of South Africa as their South African counterparts. At the same time and for many years nearly all the American and European churches continued their financial investments in South Africa. They threatened the unity of the World Council of Churches when it set up its Programme to Combat Racism, using their superior financial strength over the Third World churches to pressure compromises. The change of heart and action among the Western nations and churches has been too little and too late. The armed struggle seems to be increasingly the only way for the liberation of the oppressed in South Africa. Will the Western churches condemn the armed struggle of the oppressed in South Africa that they have helped to make inevitable through their ideological and material complicity with the apartheid regime? Not only the churches and Church Theology in South Africa stand before a *kairos,* a moment of truth. Judgment is also being passed on our churches in the West and their theology. In it they run the danger of being revealed as communities of practice who do not imitate the praxis of Jesus but that of the "ruler of this world," "the father of lies," in short, the devil.

Notes

1. José Comblin, *The Church and the National Security State* (Maryknoll, N.Y.: Orbis, 1979), pp. 79–88.

2. Stanley Hauerwas, *A Community of Character: Toward a Constructive Social Ethic* (Notre Dame: Univ. of Notre Dame Press, 1981).

3. For the central role of the Day of Covenant in Afrikaner religious ideology, see the several references in T. Dunbar Moodie, *The Rise of Afrikanerdom: Power, Apartheid and the Afrikaner Civil Religion* (Berkeley: Univ. of California Press, 1975).

4. See Norman K. Gottwald, *The Tribes of Yahweh: A Sociology of the Religion of Liberated Israel, 1250–1050 B.C.E.* (Maryknoll, N.Y.: Orbis, 1979).

5. James H. Cone, *Black Theology and Black Power* (New York: Seabury, 1969).

6. Dietrich Bonhoeffer, *Ethics,* ed. Eberhard Bethge, trans. N. H. Smith (New York: Macmillan Co., 1955), p. 17 (quoted in Cone, *Black Theology and Black Power,* p. 140f,).

9

Malusi Mpumlwana

"A crisis is a moment of truth
that shows us up for what we really are..."

— KAIROS DOCUMENT, Chap. One

It is fascinating to observe people pulling the Kairos Document apart, talking about it as a major theological statement. At home it came across as a different exercise.

I live about a thousand miles or so from where the Kairos Document was formulated. I serve as a priest in a township that has had a lot of problems. There is a place called Crossroads that is always in the news (burning here, squatters there, etc.). That's part of my area of ministry. Beyond that is an area of fruit farms that have a system of remuneration where people are given crude wine as part of their payment. Most African men going to work in that area may not bring their families. And so there are a lot of hostels. The area has the largest concentration of migrant workers outside Johannesburg. And it's the first part of the country to have a hostel dweller association.

The people developed a strong resistance to the administration and government of our country. And people just began to say that they had had enough. That is what is happening in South Africa. But the churches were not able to respond to this. They were not able to say how the gospel speaks to a situation where the people are saying that they don't want to have any more of this kind of government. We have been used to a situation where trained

---

Malusi Mpumlwana is a priest of the Church of the Province of Southern Africa.

ministers speak the gospel, marry the lovers, and bury the dead. Basically that's all that is done in our kind of pastoral ministry.

When people suddenly come around and say that they no longer want to live in the way that they have been living, we in the churches don't have a message for them. Ministers are not trained to cope with problems of this nature. We have trained people to say at funerals that God gives and God has taken; the Lord's name be praised. And suddenly we find we have to bury ten, twelve, fifteen people who have been shot mercilessly by the military in the township. And we can't say that this is God's will. Suddenly we begin to find a different type of language.

Four Eastern Cape leaders were abducted and killed and their cars were burned — we believe by the police. When this happened there was a wave of anger among the people. A lot of people left their township to go to the funeral. On the day of the funeral the state of emergency was begun in South Africa. People returning from that funeral were accosted by the military. Those who got back to the township were up to their ears with anger, and we as ministers in that township did not know how to relate to this. We had been agonizing over these problems, but somehow we always thought that this was just another crisis that would spill over and subside.

And so the Kairos Document came as a statement of reflection; it came to my part of the country saying, "Hey, we are also struggling with the same problem, and we are having meetings ourselves and talking among ourselves about how we can best respond to these issues."

The document analyzed the problem in terms of what the church is actually doing in the country. And those of us who believed ourselves to be prophetic theologians, in our own way, suddenly discovered that we were harboring very, very deep feelings of Church Theology. In fact we were liberals who were unable to formulate a theology or a ministry that is prophetic. The document was speaking to us in three different ways:

First of all, it was saying to us that we needed to sort ourselves out. Who are we? Are we advocates of State Theology? Are we advocates of Church Theology? Are we advocates of Prophetic Theology? In other words are we conservatives, are we liberals, or are we radicals who really want to have a radical transformation of our society? And when this happened we went into disarray.

Some would say, okay, I'll go along with a good deal of Prophetic Theology, but I think there are limits.

The second way the document addressed us was to ask, who are we ministering to? Who are the people that need our ministering? The people we deal with are usually benign and not likely to threaten us. They are likely to call us father and treat us nicely and give us tea in their homes. But if we wanted to get into Prophetic Theology really and truly, those people would become more radical about their own situation. This is a challenge coming from the younger people who are saying that either the church becomes a church of transformation or it's no church at all for us. Suddenly we found ourselves having to relate to a different audience that in many ways was outside the everyday congregation that we were dealing with.

The third way the document addressed us was to ask us to what extent we were willing to move the whole distance ourselves. Now this is not easy because most pastors are "middle-class" people, in that we developed middle-class values, we were trained in Western seminaries, we imbibed those values of courteousness, of etiquette. And we were challenged to develop a different way of being. We began to own the Kairos Document for ourselves and reflect on it and send back our own message to it. And it is in this context that we became signatories to the Kairos Document. The moment we started getting into this analysis we realized that the problem we were meeting was greater than just the South African government, greater than just the church structure of our synod. It was in fact the whole liberal ethos that pervades the Western world. And so the American public and the American people have become relevant for us.

The problems that we are confronting in South Africa are a spillover of problems of the whole world. And so we depend very much on the cooperation and the collaboration and the support of Christians in the rest of the Western world. What this means is that we expect you to respond to the Kairos Document in terms of what you think it means for you in North America. What structures in your country make the life of the people of South Africa more difficult? What policies in your country are complicating factors for the liberation of South Africa? If we are going to be prophetic we need to formulate strategies that will address these issues specifically.

The process becomes a pilgrimage for you as much as it is a pilgrimage for us. We cannot just say, yes, we are with the Kairos Document. We'll make a statement and endorse it and go on happily. Rather, having accepted this challenge, what does it mean in terms of our everyday activities? What does it mean in terms of our lives as Christians from week to week, from month to month? What solidarity are we building among ourselves as committed people? What are our goals from year to year? This is how it challenges us, and I would like to believe that the same kind of challenge can happen here.

The World Council of Churches (WCC) has made all kinds of very important statements about problems in the Third World. But the problem with the WCC is that it becomes a body where the liberal churches of the world deposit their consciences and sit back. It becomes a way of rinsing the consciences of the liberal world. We need to forget the statements of the WCC and get into the pilgrimage ourselves. And this is costly.

You are going to need our prayers, our love, more than we need yours. I'm not trying to belittle what you are trying to do for us. I am trying to say that I appreciate the problems that you are going to go through.

10

Josiah Young

"There are circumstances
when physical force may be used... "

— KAIROS DOCUMENT, 3.3

In its critique of Church Theology, the Kairos Document says that Church Theology "has not developed a social analysis that would enable it to understand the mechanics of injustice and oppression" (3.4). I believe, however, that Church Theology in South Africa does not avoid social analysis. The praxis of Church Theology implicitly nurtures apartheid, analyzing the political economy through paradigms of moderation. Church Theology, then, quasi-heretically condones apartheid in terms of its liberal ambivalence toward the black oppressed.

The apocalyptic meaning of the struggle against apartheid forbids liberal, ambivalent Church Theology as well as Broderbond theology. We must say no to all theologies standing in the way of the truth of the gospel.

The gospel is the story common to Christians, but the diverse meanings produced from the story are due to different hermeneutics. Whose hermeneutics most authentically surrender the truth of the gospel in South Africa? The hermeneutics of the black oppressed most authentically surrender the truth of the gospel. Positions in opposition to that truth, whether implicit or explicit, are not only exegetically incorrect, but also existentially inept. Correct theo-political praxis in South Africa arises from commitment to the black oppressed and revolutionary change.

Josiah Young is Assistant Professor in Religion at Colgate University.

The correctness of the dialectic of story and praxis among the black oppressed is evident as one compares their interpretation of Exodus to that of both the oppressor Afrikaner and the Church Theology that has complicity in the maintenance of apartheid. Exodus is an enduring paradigm for theo-political struggle because it discloses both God's identification with the oppressed and the destruction of the oppressor. As oppressors, how can Afrikaners and their liberal supporters claim that their use of the story of Exodus and their exploitation of oppressed blacks are correct? In its ambivalence to the fascist State Theology, Church Theology tends to support the travesty of the pro-apartheid interpretation of Exodus. Both theologies have missed the quintessential meaning of the story in the South African context. God stands against white supremacist oppressors, whether they are liberal or fascist. Mistakenly calling the so-called Bantu the non-elect, Afrikaners fail to see they suffer from a critical case of hardening of the heart. They fail to see that the elect are the so-called Bantu and that the Broderbond, implicitly in collusion with devotees of Church Theology, will drown in the determination of the majority to be free.

The failure of Church Theology to appreciate the relation of Jesus Christ to the Exodus makes its christology as heretical as that of State Theology. According to the gospel, the Son of God became a progeny of the oppressed who escaped the oppressor, not a progeny of the oppressor. State Theology has deified the merely human pseudo-messiah of Afrikaner nationalism. Insofar as Church Theology "starts from the premise that the apartheid regime in South Africa is a *legitimate authority*" (3.3), it too practices idolatry.

The real Son of God is from all eternity, but inextricable from the full humanity of the wretched of the "homelands." The pro-apartheid messiah is an Antichrist. We have no time to be ambivalent toward it. Time is running out. We either stand with the blacks' Christ of "one person one vote," or with the Antichrist of apartheid.

The Holy Spirit renews among the dust and smoke of Soweto. In the valley of State and Church Theologies there are only dry bones. If there is to be reconciliation by way of the ballot, then oppressors must want to cooperate with the Spirit in the work of sanctification. If the oppressors wish to oppose the oppressed, "Let he who is filthy be filthy still" (Rev. 22:11).

As it is, and most unfortunately, it looks like the bullet will be the means of reconciliation. I am not advocating violence, but I believe violence can be as redemptive as the cause of the African National Congress (ANC) is just. Justice is of God. Apartheid is of the devil. If Christ himself will slay the devil with the double-edged Word of retribution, then perhaps the ANC is that liberating word in the context of South Africa. Perhaps God is on the side of the guerrillas. Perhaps a new humanity stands behind the barrel of the gun that points toward the radical evil of apartheid. In a holy war against the Antichrist, the bullets of the oppressed are sanctified.

If apartheid must be destroyed by way of armed revolution, no guilt should be experienced in its destruction. Admittedly, violent destruction of human life should cause us all guilt, but destruction of a heinous system of injustice should be a labor of love. To suffer guilt in the destruction of apartheid would be to experience ambivalence in the face of evil.

We Afro-Americans must firmly denounce the willingness of the United States to cooperate with the Republic of South Africa. The two forces have together destabilized the development of South Africa in order to protect Western hegemony over the mineral richness of South Africa and Namibia. We must, as an oppressed people, support the true freedom fighters: the MPLA, SWAPO, FRELIMO, ZANU, and the ANC.* We must support them by the means that in praxis are necessary. *A lutta continua!*†

---

*Southern African liberation movements: MPLA: Popular Movement for the Liberation of Angola; SWAPO: South West Africa People's Organization; FRELIMO: Front for the Liberation of Mozambique; ZANU: Zimbabwe African National Union; ANC: African National Congress.

†Portuguese "The struggle continues!"; motto of the liberation movement in Mozambique.

11

Bible Study
by Thomas Hoyt, Jr.

"Here the Roman State becomes the servant of the dragon..."
— KAIROS DOCUMENT, 2.1

[1] And I saw a beast rising out of the sea, with ten horns and seven heads, with ten diadems upon its horns and a blasphemous name upon its head.

[2] And the beast that I saw was like a leopard, its feet were like a bear's, and its mouth was like a lion's mouth. And to it the dragon gave his power and his throne and great authority.

[3] One of its heads seemed to have a mortal wound, but its mortal wound was healed, and the whole earth followed the beast with wonder.

[4] Men worshiped the dragon, for he had given his authority to the beast, and they worshiped the beast, saying, "Who is like the beast, and who can fight against it?"

[5] And the beast was given a mouth uttering haughty and blasphemous words, and it was allowed to exercise authority for forty-two months;

[6] it opened its mouth to utter blasphemies against God, blaspheming his name and his dwelling, that is, those who dwell in heaven.

[7] Also it was allowed to make war on the saints and to conquer them. And authority was given it over every tribe and people and tongue and nation,

[8] and all who dwell on earth will worship it, every one whose name has not been written before the foundation of the world in the book of life of the Lamb that was slain.

[9] If any one has an ear, let him hear:

[10] If any one is to be taken captive, to captivity he goes; if any one slays with the sword, with the sword must he be slain. Here is a call for the endurance and faith of the saints.

[11] Then I saw another beast which rose out of the earth; it had two horns like a lamb and it spoke like a dragon.

[12] It exercises all the authority of the first beast in its presence, and makes the earth and its inhabitants worship the first beast, whose mortal wound was healed.

[13] It works great signs, even making fire come down from heaven to earth in the sight of men;

[14] and by the signs which it is allowed to work in the presence of the beast, it deceives those who dwell on earth, bidding them make an image for the beast which was wounded by the sword and yet lived;

[15] and it was allowed to give breath to the image of the beast so that the image of the beast should even speak, and to cause those who would not worship the image of the beast to be slain.

[16] Also it causes all, both small and great, both rich and poor, both free and slave, to be marked on the right hand or the forehead,

[17] so that no one can buy or sell unless he has the mark, that is, the name of the beast or the number of its name.

[18] This calls for wisdom: let him who has understanding reckon the number of the beast, for it is a human number, its number is six hundred and sixty-six. [Revelation 13:1–18 RSV]

The Kairos Document criticizes "Church Theology" as an inadequate response to the present crisis in South Africa. The situation in South Africa, it says, exemplifies "conflicts where one side is right and the other wrong. There are conflicts where one side is a fully armed and violent oppressor while the other side is defenseless and oppressed. There are conflicts that can only be described as the struggle between justice and injustice, good and evil, God and the devil. To speak of reconciling these two is not only a mistaken application of the Christian idea of reconciliation, it is a total betrayal of all that Christian faith has ever meant" (3.1). This perspective is akin to the apocalyptic one found in the book of Revelation. We are not called to accommodate ourselves to "the beast."

According to the Kairos Document, "If we wish to search the Bible for guidance in a situation where the State that is supposed to be 'the servant of God' betrays that calling and begins to serve

Satan instead, then we can study chapter 13 of the book of Revelation. Here the Roman State becomes the servant of the dragon (the devil) and takes on the appearance of a horrible beast" (2.1).

The book of Revelation is a graphic rendering of the scriptural theme of hope: unjust structures are changed, the persecuted are vindicated, and the persecutors are condemned and judged accordingly. This Bible study is about those who express hope in the midst of persecution; it is for those who criticize a Church Theology that tries to accommodate itself to and reform unjust structures rather than change them radically.

Apocalyptic Crisis

The apocalyptic genre of the Bible's last book makes it extremely difficult to interpret. Persons like John, who had apocalyptic visions, probably were thoroughly at home with apocalyptic literature and traditions. The imagery and symbols of this literature are rich and diverse; many have been traced to ancient Babylon and Persia. The apocalyptists drew on these materials in order to interpret their times, which called for dramatic symbols. The Revelation of John used such symbols to disclose the deeper meaning of the situation of the church in the world.

Crucial to the apocalyptic perspective is the belief that the struggles of the faithful on earth are part of a cosmic conflict between God and anti-God, an old motif. In the visionary experience, these invisible heavenly realities become visible so that the seer can interpret what is happening, or is about to happen, on earth. Apocalyptic writers did not predict events that were to happen centuries later; they dealt with the crises of their own times.

Revelation 13 comes in the central section of Revelation (11:19–16:20). Satan, the dragon, is defeated in heaven at the exaltation of Christ and thrown down to the earth (12:7–12). There, on earth, he continues the battle aimed at those who would worship God and his Christ. Satan calls first a beast from the sea (13:1–10) and then a beast from the land (13:11–18). We cannot identify these beasts exactly, but we can see that they use political (13:5–7) and economic power (13:16–17) to persecute and oppress. Both Satan and the beast from the sea are related to the imperial cult (13:4, 12–15). Satan's battle initiative, which enlists the imperial power with its totalitarian and religious claims, calls for "endurance" (13:10) and "wisdom" on the part of Christians (13:18). The author thus unveils the real cause and issue of the daily suffering of the Christian communities and exhorts them to be loyal to the sovereignty of the Lamb. And he promises them the victory in his vision of the lamb on Mt. Zion before the throne of God (14:1–5). The message of the Gospel is announced to the whole world (14:6, 7); accompanying it is the message of judgment on Rome/Babylon[1] (14:8) and on the imperial cult (14:9–11). Here is a call to endurance (14:12), identified as keeping the commandments of God and the faith of Jesus, and another hymn of praise (15:3–4), by which the church already acknowledges and shares in Christ's victory.

Hostility Toward Rome

It is widely held that Revelation 13 is a description of the Roman imperial cult under Domitian (A.D. 81–96). The author of Revelation is on the boundary, culturally speaking, because of his breach with the synagogue and his hostility to the surrounding Greco-Roman culture. He was excluded or had excluded himself from the two major social groupings of his region. This precarious situation was made even more difficult by the conflict between the Roman authorities and Christians. This facet of the social crisis seems to have been the crucial one, namely, the author's perception of the conflict between Rome and Christian faith and his expectation that it would intensify.

In part, the author's hostility to Rome is due to his identification with the Jews. Roman-Jewish relations were at first excellent, then suffered various strains, and finally degenerated into widespread hostility after the destruction of the temple. Even though the author may have viewed the second destruction as deserved punishment, Rome, the instrument of God's wrath, deserves and will receive even greater punishment (16:19; 17:7; 18:4–8).

Nero's prominence in Revelation as an Antichrist-like, eschatological adversary makes it likely that Nero's massacre of Christians in Rome in A.D. 64 was the other major reason for the author's hostility to Rome. It is quite possible that that event was a major occasion for the writing of Revelation even if as much as thirty years had intervened. According to Tacitus, large numbers of Christians were executed. Further, their deaths were of a particularly ostentatious and grotesque nature. Such an event, even if it were entirely local and unique, would have made a profound and enduring impression on Christians throughout the empire.

It is unlikely that Nero or the senate issued a general law against Christianity as such. Two other factors probably prompted Nero to act: traditional Roman rejection of foreign cults and popular hatred of Christians. Nero may have expressed some legal grounds for his action, but the nature of the charge is debated. So Nero's action and its legal basis may have set a precedent for other Roman authorities who followed him. Or they may have taken analogous actions independently, perhaps under popular pressure. When Pliny encountered Christians in Bithynia about A.D. 112, he concluded that it was his duty to execute any unrepentant, adult, male Christian who was properly accused.[2] Again, the charge is not completely clear, but the general effect certainly is.

The major grounds for the author's perception of a Roman threat then are the massacre of Christians by Nero in A.D. 64, the destruction of Jerusalem in A.D. 70, and the continuous danger to Christians throughout the empire.

In addition to these general factors, a particular, local event probably played a role in creating the author's sense of crisis. This was the death of Antipas in Pergamum (2:13). The circumstances of his death are not given clearly by the text. That he is called a witness (martyr) implies that he died for his Christian faith. In this context, his death is closely associated with "Satan's throne." In light of Chapters 12–13, Satan's throne must be understood in terms of Roman power. Thus, it is likely that Antipas was executed by the order of the provincial governor. Why was the author himself banished rather than executed? The most probable explanation is that he claimed to be and was recognized as a Jew, who was then banished for practicing magic.

Can Satanic States Perform Wonders?

While many scholars have looked at Revelation in the light of images from the Old Testament, there is some relevance in approaching Revelation in the light of actual historical occurrences in the first century. Steven J. Scherrer has helped immensely in our understanding the manner in which Roman government solidified its imperial power through signs and wonders.[3] He contends that Revelation 13:13–15 describes the actual cult of the rulers in the East.

It is quite plausible that technology and simulation of nature were employed in the imperial cult.

It has been long recognized that Revelation 13 is a thinly veiled polemic — using language from Daniel 7 — against the Roman imperial cult. In apocalyptic tradition, evil emerges from the sea, the symbol of chaos. In Daniel 7, four beasts come from the sea: a lion, a bear, a leopard, and one so dreadful that it cannot be compared with any animal. These beasts represent the sequence of empires: (probably) the Babylonian, the Medean, the Persian, and the Greek. The same theme is expressed in Revelation 13: the beast from the sea is an empire, Rome. Revelation 13:1–2 combines elements of the beasts in Daniel 7 because John believes that in Rome all evils in the past came to a head. This beast from the sea receives the dragon's power, that is, Rome rules by satanic power.

According to Revelation 13:4, people worship the beast because they are awed by its power. The beast blasphemes God, an allusion to emperor worship in general and to Domitian's claim that he is lord and god. Specifically, God allows the beast to persecute the church, but only for a limited time (symbolized by an exact number). In the midst of persecution the church should know that God is in charge, despite appearances to the contrary.

There were many appearances to the contrary. One sees the awesome power of Rome, for example, when the lion that is a lamb opens the seven seals (chapters 6–8). Four aspects of Roman rule and power are revealed: military expansionism, civil strife and war, inflation (which robs the poor of sustenance), and death. The fifth seal displays another image of Roman rule in that the martyrs cry out to the Lord for judgment and vindication. The way of the imperial cult is that of idolatry, murder, sorcery, immorality, and theft (9:20). Yet God will reign supreme over those who are "the destroyers of the earth." God protects and saves the earth, not only the "prophets and saints," but all who repent and fear God's name (11:18).

Revelation 13:11–18 introduces a second beast. The two beasts presented in Revelation 13 represent respectively the Roman Imperium, introduced in 13:1–2, and the political-cultic personnel connected with its cultus on the local level. The second beast arises from the land, that is, locally (v. 11). The first beast is its source of authority (v. 12); the second beast forces the population to make an image of the first beast (v. 14) and to worship it

(v. 15). The second beast is the imperial priesthood, which promotes emperor worship. The State must have functionaries to do its bidding.

In Revelation 13:13–15, the imperial cult of Rome is said to perform religious wonders. The "great signs" are (1) "making fire come down from heaven to earth in the sight of men" (v. 13); and (2) giving "breath to the image of the beast so that the image of the beast should even speak" (v. 15). These signs could be part of the mythological imagery of chapter 13 as a whole, which can speak of the empire, for example, as a "beast rising out of the sea, with ten horns and seven heads, with ten diadems upon its horns and a blasphemous name upon its heads" (v. 1), or can speak of the local cult officials as a "beast which rose out of the earth," having horns like a lamb, but speaking like a dragon (v. 11). Indications are, however, that verses 13–15 should be taken as something more than mythological imagery. We seem to be dealing with actual phenomena in the imperial cult.

It may be possible that John is constructing his report of signs and wonders out of the tradition behind Mark 13:22: "false Christs and false prophets will arise and show signs and wonders, to lead astray, if possible, the elect"; it seems unlikely, however, that John would invent powerful and impressive miracles and attribute them to his archrival and opponent were there no evidence whatsoever for their existence. Furthermore, contrived religious wonders were not unusual in the ancient world, but nowhere, except in Revelation 13:13–15, are they attested as part of the imperial cult as such.

According to many texts from the second century, there was a general readiness on the part of many people to believe that certain statues under certain conditions could speak and move and display fire through manipulation or through the power of Satan. The historical basis for the description of signs and wonders as practiced by the state functionaries is found in the deceptive technological practices of such persons as the second-century cultist Alexander the false prophet, written of by Lucian. Alexander had the ability to make an image that appeared to be alive. He even displayed the body and tail of a real serpent, which seemed to be that of the artificial head.

In other words, there were functionaries in the Roman imperial cult who probably fooled the people to the extent that they coaxed from them worship of the imperial state on the basis of these signs and wonders. The difference between Lucian's and John's account is that Lucian attributes these signs to mere trickery while John apparently believes the wonders are real but that Satan is behind them. By way of summary, we can say that in the first century the imperial cult of the State actually manipulated images or belief in them in order to induce awe and worship.

Who is 666?

A great deal of scholarly work has concentrated upon the meaning of the number 666 (13:18). People have offered many names for the person represented by that number. To understand the suggestions made on the basis of numbers, we must remember that before the Arabs gave us our numbers, Greeks, Romans, and Jews counted with letters. If we do this in English, then $a = 1$, $b = 2$, $c = 3$, etc. With such a system one can count names. All kinds of combinations can add up to 666.

Two possibilities are of special interest. We can spell Neron Kaisar in Hebrew, and then add up the name to get 666. On this basis, the number would mean that Nero, the evil torturer, had returned, as some thought he would. Or we can add up the abbreviation of Domitian's titles that he put on coins. On this basis, the number refers to Domitian himself. Actually, it is not clear that John had only one meaning in mind. Most scholars, however, think that Nero is meant in this context.

The fact that Domitian was probably emperor at the time of John's writing presents no serious problem. It was traditional for apocalyptists to repeat material from earlier times without recasting them or contemporizing them. Although the identity of the figure hidden behind the number cannot be known, the intent of the symbol is clear; it is a veiled allusion to an emperor claiming divine status, in all probability Domitian.

A caution must be offered. Since John used this numeral in only one verse, the obsession with decoding the number 666 often leads to a gross distortion of emphasis. He is greatly concerned with the power of the beast, but does not rely upon this numeral alone to convey his message to his original readers.

Patient Endurance

The vision of the beast from the earth in 13:11–18 depicts the crisis that Christians faced. In verses 16–17 it is said that this beast from the earth creates a situation in which no one can buy or sell unless one has the mark, the name of the beast, or the number of its name. On one level, the mark of the beast is symbolic, an intangible sign that corresponds to the seal of God (7:3; 4:4). In this passage, where the author is speaking of the cult of the ruler of his own day and where much of the chapter fits quite nicely with other contemporary events and practices, the image of the "mark" takes on connotations of the author's contemporary situation and expresses his dilemma.

Here the reference to buying and selling calls to mind the portrait, name, and other characteristics of the emperor that appeared on Roman coins of the time. The Christian is thus faced with the alternative of acknowledging imperial claims to divinity by use of the coins or virtual separatism and economic boycott. The threat of eternal punishment for those who receive the mark of the beast (14:9–11) implies that the author of Revelation is calling for such a boycott.

The task of the persecuted community is not to do battle with the sword but to bear faithful witness and to persevere in suffering: "Whoever is to be made prisoner, a prisoner shall he be. Whoever takes the sword to kill, by the sword he is bound to be killed. This is where the fortitude and faithfulness of God's people have their place" (Rev. 13:10 NEB). In the book of Revelation, the oppressed community was not to take matters into its own hands by resorting to fighting. (How we apply this injunction in the South African context will be determined by our view of Scripture; cf. the Kairos Document, 3.3.) In Revelation, judgment on the enemies of God is reserved solely for the returning Christ.

Patient endurance is not passivity. This resistance movement, this counter-empire, does not take up arms to achieve power. The Christians do not plot a coup to seize economic and political control. But even in their style of resistance, they are to give testimony to the victory of the Lamb that was slain and to the transformation of economic and political power effected by him. They are to defend the Lord's claim to an earth corrupted and abused by its alliance with Satan and the emperor. They are to live courageously and faithfully, resisting the pollutions of the cult of the emperor, including its murder, fornication, sorcery, idolatry, and especially its lie that Caesar is Lord (see the lists in 21:8; 22:15; 9:20, 21). All of life is to be lived under the sovereignty of the true Lord. "Patient endurance" is not a retreat from the ethical dimension but the introduction to it, for conventional, legal, and prudential standards are all overridden by what one really ought to do — submit to the rule of God. The prophet by his visions and the churches by their counter-empire existence bear witness to that rule and are tokens of its realization for the whole earth.

The End of the State

While details and their meanings are unclear in Revelation 12–13, one thing is clear: John regards Rome as evil (in chapter 17, Rome is called the Great Whore). The vision of Babylon/Rome and the fall of Rome (17:1–19:10) describes the great magnificence of Rome, at which even the seer marveled (17:6). Rome flaunts its wealth and power, but this does not hide its immorality and idolatry. Roman oppression and murder, and therefore God's judgment, are unveiled (18:1–8, 21–24). The fall of Babylon/Rome is lamented by those who were powerful and wealthy according to standards of Rome and with Roman aid: "the kings of the earth" (18:9–10), "the merchants" (18:11–17a) and "the shipmasters" (18:17b–19), those who share in the power. The certainty of Babylon's fall and the Lord's victory, however, is cause for celebration and exhortation among God's people. They rejoice (18:20) and already join in the heavenly "hallelujah" (19:1, 3, 6) even as they heed the call for a spiritual exodus: "come out of her, my people" (18:4). The exodus required is from the demonic values, the pride of power (18:3, 9, 10), and the greed (18:3, 11–19) that marked Rome's life and justified the doom of Rome. Such a spiritual exodus could be undertaken only in the assurance of the victory of the Lamb that was slain, who judges justly and makes war for righteousness (19:11), becoming "the King of kings and Lord of lords" (19:16). Such a spiritual exodus could be undertaken only in the expectation of a new world and a new city: "the holy city, new Jerusalem" (21:2), where God dwells and reigns and blesses and where God's creation and people flourish. Such a spiritual exodus requires and enables "patient endurance."

According to Revelation, the destruction of the godless power and its accomplices happens miraculously in a "final battle." The returning Christ appears here, in total conformity with Jewish models, as the Warrior Messiah on a white horse; "from his mouth issues a sharp sword with which to smite the nations" (Rev. 19:15). The depiction of the bloody annihilation of all God's enemies shows the animosity, indeed the hatred, the seer has for the power of Rome:

> And I saw the beast and the kings of the earth with their armies gathered to make war against him who sits upon the horse and against his army. And the beast was captured, and with it the false prophet who in its presence had worked the signs by which he deceived those who had received the mark of the beast and those who worshiped its image. These two were thrown alive into the lake of fire that burns with sulphur. And the rest were slain by the sword of him who sits upon the horse, the sword that issues from his mouth; and all the birds were gorged with their flesh. (Rev. 19:20–21)

Thus ends the power of the beast. In the words of the Kairos Document, "God will not permit his unfaithful servant to reign forever" (2.1).

Notes

1. Like IV Ezra, II Baruch, and Sibylline Oracles, the book of Revelation refers to Rome with the symbolic name "Babylon." The use of this name probably had a variety of connotations, but the major reason for its use is surely the correspondence between the two cities as the first and second destroyers of Jerusalem and the temple.

2. Pliny, *Epistles* 10.96. See J. Stevenson, ed. *A New Eusebius* (London: SPCK, 1963), p. 13.

3. See Steven J. Scherrer, "Signs and Wonders in the Imperial Cult: A New Look at a Roman Religious Institution in the Light of Rev. 13:13–15," *Journal of Biblical Literature* 103/4 (1984), pp. 599–610.

Part Four
PROPHETIC THEOLOGY

12

Cornel West

*"...our theology must name the sins and evils that surround us
and the salvation that we are hoping for..."*

— Kairos Document, 4.1

The Kairos Document is a call to action and for solidarity from oppressed Christians in the belly of one beast to us Christians in the belly of another beast. And the link between those beasts has to be part of our investigation. Prophetic Theology cuts much deeper than the intellect; Prophetic Theology forces us to exemplify in our own lives what we espouse in our rhetoric. It raises questions of integrity, questions of character, and, most importantly, questions of risk and sacrifice. One of the things that inspires me about the South African theologians and Christians is that they are caught in a whirlwind, so that, like in the early church, to be a Christian means to risk and to sacrifice.

In South Africa it is a crime to hope; to be a serious Christian is to commit a crime, just as for the early Christians to be a Christian meant to end up in the lion's den. And this is in many ways alien to us First World Christians. In our post-modern culture, a culture of deathlessness, of surfaces, of commodities, commitment itself becomes a commodity. Commitment itself becomes fashionable. Some even make careers on it. One of the things that I learned in my visit to South Africa in the summer of 1985 was that to be a Christian, in a serious sense, means that you have to come to terms with death.

Cornel West is Professor of Philosophy and Christian Practice at Union Theological Seminary, New York.

So Prophetic Theology goes far, far beyond the kind of disciplinary division of labor that we see within our academic institutions. We're talking about living a certain kind of life. Some of our grandmothers understand this. We young folk, in many instances, have to be called back, and ironically called back by young heroes in South Africa who are willing to give their lives, to sacrifice, and to do it daily.

We find three basic components in Prophetic Theology. The first is a religious conception of what it is to be human, of how we are to act, of what we are to hope for. We'll put this under the rubric of *religious vision.*

The second crucial component is *historical and social analysis,* which is simply a set of tools or intellectual analytical weapons that help us in a struggle. The context is a battlefield, struggle, resistance, contestation.

The third component is *action,* what will we do? Lord, what will you have us to do? We must name our action, praxis, strategies, tactics.

Religious Vision

We begin with *imago Dei,* being made in the image of God. Can we take seriously the radical egalitarian implication of the notion that God made all human beings in God's image and that therefore all individuals are unique and distinctive and have a sanctity and dignity of their own, that they therefore have equal status and warrant a particular type of treatment? The doctrine of *imago Dei* is, on the one hand, radically egalitarian. On the other hand it is radically universalistic, but is targeted on those who are denied dignity and a certain minimum of humane treatment.

The very notion of humane treatment is inseparable from historical struggle. Humane treatment four hundred years ago was very different from what it is now. But it means a Christian mandate for identification with the downtrodden, the dispossessed, the disinherited, with the exploited and the oppressed. The doctrine of *imago Dei* also accents individuals, individuals in community. It means that individuals are never reducible to community. It holds at arm's length any authoritarian communitarianism and it promotes a healthy communitarianism. Individuals are unintelligible without the community, but the individual is irreducible to the community as well. We all die by ourselves. We all struggle with despair and dread, each in our own way. In this complex dialectical interplay between individual and community we must not lose sight of our religious vision.

A second dimension of our religious vision is fallenness, the doctrine of sin. We are finite and fallen and therefore there ought to be institutional mechanisms that insure that fallen human beings not abuse their power. Lord Acton is right: absolute power corrupts absolutely. Radical democracy is the best we finite, fallen creatures can do. Democracy is an ethical implication of the Christian conception of what it is to be human. The question is how we understand democracy. What is its content? What is its substance?

The third dimension of our religious vision has to do with the coming of the kingdom, with the empowerment that flows from the inbreaking and invading of a kingdom that on the one hand is beyond our power and on the other is inseparable from what we can do. We are kingdom-bound. We are never kingdom-creating, but we stay in contact with its power. People tend to think that religious talk is different from political talk. You can talk about a kingdom, but it's just a metaphor, just an image. No, it's very real. You have to have deep, deep religious faith to stay in the struggle for a long time. Ask anybody who's been in the struggle for a long time. You have to have deep faith. For Christians it means digging deep into the depths of what kingdom-talk is about. That's our only source of empowerment.

If you haven't dealt with the bondage of death and despair, then you're going to be disillusioned, just like all secular lefters who struggle for five years and then go live the good life. They haven't dug deep enough. This is not a sprint; this is a marathon. The Kairos Document understands that. So when we talk about kingdom, we talk about empowerment. We talk about something that fundamentally impinges upon those who are attempting to be serious Christians. I like the talk about hope in the Kairos Document. We live in a time when hope itself has been called into question as a category. That's why the cynicism is so pervasive. Possibility itself is called into question. That's what it means to live at the end of the age of Europe and in the middle of the Americanization and Sovietization of the world.

Anybody who takes hope seriously and possibility seriously is going to look like a fool in our world. Weber talked about the world as an iron cage. Adorno talks about the iron cage in Marxist terms. They call hope in question. Often they invoke holocaust to describe the evil in the midst of a civilized Europe. The holocaust is one of the grand evils of human history, yet it doesn't impose a closure on hope. It might for those who have a parochial vision, a Eurocentric vision, more than for those who have been dealing with many holocausts down through the corridors of time.

Historical and Social Analysis

The second component of Prophetic Theology accented by the Kairos Document is historical and social analysis. I cannot over-emphasize how important this analysis is. But I'm not making an ideal of it; it is only a weapon. It is important because there is a sense in which everybody these days agrees on values. Botha and Reagan claim to be for freedom; I'm for freedom; you're for freedom. But if everybody agrees on values, why do we have these fundamental conflicts? When I debate Michael Novak and other Christian neoconservatives, we all step up and talk about how we're for democracy, we're for liberty, we're for freedom. And then he goes on to support the U.S. invasion in Nicaragua. The difference is that in many instances we have a different historical and social analysis. We understand power differently. We understand wealth differently. We understand the circulation of influence and prestige differently. And so the battle within the Christian tradition is often a battle over which historical and social analysis we are deploying. The question is whether that analysis is informed by a Christocentric perception, informed by the cross — capital *c* — as well as the many crosses — small *c* — that people have to bear everyday.

Historical and social analysis means that we have to have some sense of the larger context, the larger forces that shape and mold not only who we are but our projection of where we want to go. Again there are three points I want to mention here. The first has to do with the Europeanization of the world. The age of Europe began in 1492. It reached its peak in the nineteenth and early twentieth centuries. By Europe I mean the handful of nations between the Atlantic Ocean and the Ural mountains. In 1835 they owned 35 percent of the globe, and by 1918 they owned 87 percent of the globe. This went hand in hand with the subjugation of non-

European peoples as well as the exploitation of European workers. That is the backdrop of what we're dealing with. It is inseparable from the emergence of the capitalist mode of production, social relations of production, the creation of various classes in which one class owns the land and instruments of production and the majority of human beings are forced to sell themselves like commodities, that is, sell their time, their energy, and their skills in order to stay alive. In the nineteenth century if you didn't find a job you starved. These conditions of industrial market capitalism have changed only after the tremendous, protracted struggles of oppressed people.

There is a small dose of humanity within First World capitalism. But when we look at the Third World we can see just what capitalism once looked like, because there it is still ugly and brutish and nasty and oppressive. What is distinctive in many ways about South Africa is that it still maintains the legacy and the residue of the Europeanization of the world, because it is still an old colonial regime. Europe was in decline and the United States and the Soviet Union began to emerge. But in South Africa we can still see indigenous people. The United States is not vastly different, because the United States, like Australia and Canada, is a European settler society too. U.S. experience began with the dispossession of people's land, extermination, genocide. Just go to a reservation to be reminded of American history from a point of view different from that of the mainstream. In South Africa the indigenous population was able to resist, and they were rendered useful as cheap labor. They are still there and they aren't going anywhere. They continue to resist. It is an old legacy.

By the 1970s most of Africa had begun to burst out of the older form of Europeanization, though we know it continues in neocolonial forms. We in the United States recognize that our country, like South Africa, had to engage in an anticolonial and anti-imperialistic struggle against Britain. That is one of the ironies of being an American. There is a sense in which the United States, the nation born modern, born liberal, born bourgeois, was once a revolutionary country, even as it subjugated people of African descent. The Declaration of Independence sounds revolutionary. They were talking not only about a change within a government, but the human power to change fundamentally the structures of government themselves. That's what the slavemaster Jefferson wrote about. He had revolutionary blood flowing in some parts of his veins. We won't talk about the other parts, in relation to his slaves. But there is an important revolutionary tradition in what is now one of the major counter-revolutionary powers in the world. A similar process occurred in South Africa. The Afrikaners struggled against British imperialism and then subjected the indigenous populations to subjugation.

There is no doubt in my mind that if the South had won the Civil War, there would still be apartheid in the South. In fact for the most part we had apartheid up until 1964: the crypto-fascist terrorism, the institutionalized racism, the lynching, that strange fruit that southern trees bore and Billy Holliday sang so poignantly about. It would all still be here if it were not for the penetration of capital from the North and the emergence of liberal elites within a Democratic party that began opening itself to the movement of Martin Luther King, Jr., and others. Apartheid is not far removed from the American experience. The parallels have much to say to us.

Dealing then with historical and social analysis as tools, as weapons, we begin to look at other institutional forms that deny life. I have talked about economics, but we can also talk about the repression of the State. State repression occurs not only in South Africa. The population of our prisons is 47 percent black and brown, but blacks represent only 11 percent of the population, and our brown brothers and sisters only another 7 percent. South Africa is up against one of the most brutal apparatuses known to humankind. It is a counterinsurgency State that specializes in smashing insurgents. We could point to Chile and Korea as well. This State repression goes hand in hand with economic exploitation. Look at the response to strikes in South Africa. It looks like Rockefeller in 1877. Rockefeller had a vigilante group bigger than the state military in Ohio. The U.S. had a very weak state from 1877 to 1920. That's one of the reasons we had robber barons and tremendous consolidation of wealth.

When South Africans go on strike, the repressive apparatus comes down. But you cannot rule a society solely by force. You can attempt to, but over time you need something else. You either have to convince the people to consent to their oppression or you have to attempt to marginalize those who refuse to consent. Even the repressive State apparatus in South Africa cannot rule by sheer force; the Kairos Document is an example of that. Like the

Confessing Church in Nazi Germany, the Kairos Document shows that the human spirit refuses to be completely snuffed out. Those of us who are Christian believe this has something to do with the God we worship, with the grounds of hope so foolish in the eyes of many.

My second point in relation to historical and social analysis is *racism*. Racism is inseparable from economic exploitation and State repression, but it is not identical to them. Racism has its own specificity. The white European supremacist practices that are institutionalized in the everyday life of South Africans and are still often operative in this country have their own life and logic. They are related to but are not subsumable under the economy. Racism is embodied in the child's question, Why do white folks treat black folks so bad? Some say that this is an anachronistic question: It used to be the case, but we've undergone tremendous progress. I say no, we have to keep asking the question.

Africans understand what it is to be culturally and esthetically degraded and devalued by non-Africans. The degradation works on a personal level and has to do with identity and subjectivity, with how you conceive of yourself, with whether you have the capacity or whether you think you have the capacity to affirm your own potential. We see this every day in black children.

Third, we must mention the *subjugation of women*. Patriarchal practices, the degrading and devaluating and the marginalizing, pervade all other practices. One might raise the so-called women's question within both First World and Third World contexts. But the women's question is not a strategic question, it is a Christian one. If we talk about evil, we're going to talk about subjugation. Don't shy away from evil if you're a Christian. Look at it for what it is and try to come to terms with it. And ask the Lord Christ to empower you to struggle against it.

Action

To be a Christian is fundamentally to live a certain kind of life, to live a sacrificial life, a love-informed life, a life of care and a life of giving. The question then becomes how to live a Christian life in a context in which the class and race contradictions are so intense that there is civil war. How do you live in that kind of brokenness? This is one of the questions I see emerging from the Prophetic Theology of the Kairos Document. And the crucial question then becomes, What are the alternatives? What are the options? None of us is born under circumstances of our own choosing, whether in the biological sense or in the familial sense. The scope of our options will be very different depending on our context. The United States presents a certain set of options, still very, very limited. How do you deal with a two-party system that is basically run by the economic and political elites of the country. What kind of progressive alternatives are there? Do you work on the local level and struggle with Brother Harold Washington in Chicago? Can there be more Washingtons across the country and less Bradleys? An important question. Bradley's still better than the alternative in Los Angeles. This shows you how bad things are.

The context in South Africa is even more limited and more intense because the blood flows more freely. Raise the issue of armed struggle with First World Christians and they usually tend to shake a bit, as if they didn't have a history of armed struggle, as if their ancestors didn't fight in the anti-capitalist armed guerrilla Revolutionary War of America in 1776 or in the Civil War in 1860. As if they didn't go marching off to World War I and couldn't wait to march off to World War II. Don't talk about armed struggle to oppressed people until you understand your own history.

On the other hand armed struggle is no plaything either. It reminds us of just how tragic the human condition can actually be. I have great respect for non-violent leaders like Martin Luther King, Jr., Allan Boesak, and others. I don't agree with them, but I have great respect for them. I think that those within the Christian tradition who unequivocally refuse to accept violence advocate a respectable position, although not persuasive to me. I think those who hold this position play a role, but I don't think they are going to be major agents in the making of history. They represent a moral position that reminds us of how tragic our situation is. But given the tragedy it seems to me that there certainly are circumstances in which Christians ought to engage in armed struggle. I can certainly envision myself doing so. I believe that we should never advocate any position that we are not willing to accept ourselves.

To accept armed struggle the situation has to be extreme. All alternatives have to be exhausted and you have to be able to point to historical evidence that they are exhausted. Most importantly you have to be able to point to the probable success of armed struggle. It cannot be simply adolescent rebellion. It has to be worked out, with detailed and elaborate strategies and tactics. George Washington understood this. There might be a point, in various parts of the globe including South Africa, where Christians will be forced to engage in armed struggle. Far be it from me to pontificate on this from Chicago; I'm simply raising the possibility.

There are other forms of struggle as well. The role of the church is in the community organizations. One thinks of course of the United Democratic Front and other such groups. The role of the church can vary. In the United States the church has a crucial role in various local progressive organizations. These days such organizations are not very popular, but they can continue to hold the line so that maybe by the 1990s, when things begin to be shaken up again, these organizations can emerge just as they did in the 1950s.

The last point of political strategy is the role of labor. I think in South Africa this is especially important because of the central role of industrial workers and the contribution that their organization can make to community action groups. In the United States the issue of labor is different, but still very important. As we undergo deindustrialization, the high-tech revolution, the new collar and white collar and brown collar revolutions, labor takes on a very different configuration. It becomes much more heterogeneous, much more diverse. This means that there will be different ways and different patterns in which organizing moves. Blacks, browns, and women will more and more become the cutting edge of the labor movement, linked in interracial solidarity. Where are our churches in relation to our progressive trade unions? That's one thing we can learn from both South Africa and the Kairos Document. We must refuse to give up the best of those long traditions of struggle, often times in flawed ways, for democracy, for justice.

I hope that the Kairos Document inspires the First World, North America, that it infuses us with the depth of commitment that is displayed by the pen put to paper of that document. There is a sense in which American culture is becoming more and more a kind of wasteland, a wasted possibility, an unrealized potentiality. We are in deep need of inspiration. We are in deep need of seeing human beings, and especially Christians, in social motion. There will be no change in America, there will be no change in South

Africa, there will be no change in Chile or Nicaragua, until there are human beings in social motion. The possibility of social motion is kept alive by the grand gift that has been given to us. The gift of the Kairos Document is another form of God's empowerment for us to continue to struggle.

13

Peter Walshe

*"... a Prophetic Theology would include a reading
of the signs of the times."*

— KAIROS DOCUMENT, 4.1

There is a long-term evolutionary process working its way through
political communities around the globe. It is a movement of ideas
and hopes rooted in the experience of earlier centuries, some would
say dating back to the great prophets of the Jewish Scriptures.
This process is the search for a more egalitarian society, a search
that periodically expresses itself in the discomforting, prophetic
voices of brave people, such as those who drafted the Kairos Document.

Unfortunately, this struggle for justice that is taking place in all
political cultures is often repressed or muted for lengthy periods of
time, as it is in the United States today. In South Africa, however,
the history of racism and economic exploitation, the prolonged
experience of segregation and then of apartheid, has culminated
in civil war. After decades of hesitant, patient, and non-violent
protest, the struggle against apartheid and for a more egalitarian future has now become a broadly based liberation movement.
We need to see this South African struggle as part of that much
wider sweep of human history, a history of injustice and, at times,
crushing disappointments, but always of hope.

The prophetic voices within black politics and church life have
taken a long time to reach the point articulated in the Kairos
Document. Let me offer a few examples of the process. In 1912

*Peter Walshe is Director of African Studies and Professor of Government and
International Studies at the University of Notre Dame, Indiana.*

the African National Congress was formed by men and women of Christian conviction who objected to the color-bar constitution of the New Union of South Africa. They were also flabbergasted by the grotesquely unjust land division that left but 13 percent of the country for the black majority. After years of non-violent protest, moral appeals, delegations, and petitions, a tougher, resilient political will emerged: a determination to confront white power in the pursuit of justice. This more activist, prophetic mindset resulted, in part, from a final disillusionment with white power that followed upon the abolition of the Cape common voters roll in 1936. (This roll, an anachronism within the segregated political life of South Africa, permitted Africans in that province to qualify for the vote — although the constitution forbade their sitting in parliament!) The reaction of D.D.T. Jabavu, the first black professor in South Africa and a political moderate, to this renewed burst of white racism was terse: "The structure of European political morality has toppled and collapsed from above our heads to its pristine level of the jungle that obtained two thousand years ago."

From this point onward, Africans came to bear responsibility themselves for the future of South Africa. Eventually this led to the Defiance Campaigns of the 1950s and the Black Consciousness uprisings of the mid-1970s. In spite of draconian repression, this liberation movement then gathered strength in the early 1980s through the revival of the (illegal) African National Congress and the efforts of a wide range of organizations currently challenging the legitimacy of the apartheid state and its new 1983 constitution: *inter alia,* the United Democratic Front, the Congress of South African Trade Unions, the South African Council of Churches, and the South African Catholic Bishops Conference. It is this protracted struggle for a non-racist, egalitarian society, as well as the present turmoil and escalating violence, that produced the Kairos Document.

While the Kairos Document focuses on the satanic phenomenon of the apartheid system, it is important that an on-going prophetic witness be nurtured within South African Christianity, a witness that will contribute to the struggle for justice in a post-revolutionary South Africa too. This takes me to my second point: the Kairos Document appeals for a continuous, hard-nosed social analysis that is founded on the process of listening to ordinary people, those who suffer the full weight of exploitation and oppression. This listening process, which lies at the core of the Kairos methodology, should be extended to take in the experience of dispossessed people throughout tropical Africa and the frontline states. The high hopes present at independence have, in most cases, been dashed. This negative set of experiences in countries to the north should also inform the struggle for justice in South Africa itself and so help to guide the search for new forms of political participation and economic restructuring. For instance, there are issues to be faced not only in land redistribution, but in nurturing labor-intensive agriculture through various types of cooperative or commune systems. There is a crying need for a movement away from capital-intensive development strategies. New corporate structures must be encouraged too, with elements of worker ownership and/or worker control. The alternative is simply to change the color of the existing regime, to produce a new black elite in alliance with established white economic privilege.

My third point is that the Kairos Document is symptomatic of a foundational shift in the nature of legitimate government, a shift that has worldwide implications. A couple of examples will illustrate this. In traditional African societies, the king was legitimate because he inhabited a particular cosmology; he was the intermediary between the deities and ancestors, and the living population. People willingly obeyed because the king was high priest as well as chief justice, executive, and ultimate legislator. These cosmologies have been very largely destroyed by the impact of the West and colonialism. As a result, the recently created post-colonial states are in search of a new basis for legitimate government.

My second example comes from Europe. When the American colonies rebelled in 1776, and when the Bastille was stormed in the French Revolution of 1789, the foundations of the old monarchical orders were shattered and a new basis for legitimate government had to be found. At this time, the core idea of modern nationalism was forming as an alternative to divine right monarchy — the sovereignty of the people. Now, two hundred years later, we are witnessing in the Kairos Document and in the South African liberation struggle — and elsewhere, for example in Central America and the Philippines — a further shift in the nature of legitimate government. I am suggesting that governments will be legitimate in the twenty-first century, not simply because they have the support of the people, but because they are active in the redistribution of resources so as to overcome class polarization. Without such a commitment, regimes will be illegitimate — the brutally repressive instruments of established elites. The Kairos Document reminds us in a prophetic way that justice requires this egalitarian vision. Without such an inspiration, I believe, we will move into a nightmarish, George Orwellian future.

Finally, we have been asked to think about the implications of the Kairos Document for Christians outside South Africa, in particular here in the United States. What does it mean for us to be unequivocally and consistently identified with the poor and oppressed? As citizens of a superpower, I suggest we must re-examine the nature of our foreign aid programs: they are very badly skewed by ideological, cold-war thinking and do not focus on the essential need to sponsor grassroots reform among the poorest on our planet. We must also revise our foreign policy priorities and recognize that there are indigenous struggles for justice in Southern Africa, and other Third World areas, that will produce a pluralistic world with many different economic and political systems. In other words, we in the United States are called to listen to the poor of the Third World — even if their populist liberation movements espouse political and economic orders that are not replicas of our own.

14

Albert Pero

*"Prophetic Theology... will have to be infused
with a spirit of fearlessness and courage,
a spirit of love and understanding... "*

—KAIROS DOCUMENT, 4.1

"What is it," ask the Kairos theologians, "that would make our response truly prophetic? What would be the characteristics of a Prophetic Theology?" (Chap. Four).

The prophet has a high level of *sensitivity*. The prophet can read what the other person is about without words having been exchanged. For example, I learned as a little boy how to communicate with my parents without talking. This same sensitivity explains how one survives in a situation where one is prevented from audibly communicating by an alien language structure and context.

Another way of stating this is that one must learn how to communicate between the beats. We had a dance in the black community called the "bump." In this dance you "bump" your partner with your hips. We taught some of the young whites of that day to do the bump, but they had a difficult time because they could not bump on the offbeat. If you cannot communicate on the offbeat, then you are never on the beat. This being in "sync," this sensitivity of the prophet, who can walk in a room and know what you're thinking before you say it, is startling. The sensitivity that those black folks weren't supposed to have they in fact possessed all the

Albert Pero is Associate Professor of Theology and Cross Cultural Studies at Lutheran School of Theology, Chicago.

time. You only have to read the Kairos Document to see this prophetic sensitivity. Most people in those higher schools of learning for the past 350 years — knowing Hebrew, Greek, Latin, German, and all the rest of the academic curriculum — seem to have less prophetic vision than the authors of the document. Sensitivity is a gift of God.

Courage is another true mark of a prophet. I see this in the historical continuity between the Old Testament prophets' words and the words of the prophets of today. And courage is moral boldness. Courage is a unique ability to tell the truth no matter what happens. For example, if we were studying classical theology, we might approach the material with the profound question: what in the world does "confession" mean? And someone with the sensitivity of a prophet might say: "My brother or my sister, confession is proclamation in crisis!" It really has almost nothing to do with whether you go to church or recite the Apostles' Creed. It has to do with whether or not you can tell the truth in the midst of crisis. That's what confession is — proclamation in crisis!

I'm fascinated by the three "African brothers" in the Bible. They have strange names (just as Africans have funny names from the vantage point of Americans) — Shadrach, Meshach, and Abednego. They made a confession in the midst of a crisis before the person who was telling them an untruth, namely, the king. The king was saying, "Acknowledge the fact that I'm God and I'm running your life. Indeed," said the king, "I want you to acknowledge that I'm in control of life and death." And the three brothers looked at each other, I'm sure they did, and asked, "Why would he say that? He knows that we've got to tell the truth." And being the black brothers that they were, I'm sure they said something like: "Well, if you must insist on it, then take your best shot. We cannot acknowledge something that we know is not true: that you are in control of life and death." "All right then," said the king. "I'll prove it to you. I will throw you in the furnace and put you to death." You all know the end of the story. But it takes courage to resist the demonic and hold fast to faith in God.

Third, prophets have *compassion*. The compassion that I've seen throughout the biblical material and in all the prophets today is not a sentimental, anemic compassion. Prophetic compassion has an anger second to none. Some people call it "righteous indignation." But whatever it is, the compassion of the prophet is motivated by anger and is expressed in the strongest denunciation of evil.

A fourth characteristic of a prophet is *self-criticism.* What is the critique of Africans and black Americans relative to the Kairos Document? We cannot continually analyze our own oppression or even our participation with the oppressor in our own oppression without the gospel critique.

Fifth, there is a tremendous *ambiguity* within which the prophet functions. Sometimes, my brothers and sisters, it *is* hard to determine what is truly God's will for a given time.

Emmanuel Kant said something to the effect that concepts without precepts are empty and void. All these formulations without action are indeed like necrophilia, that is, a love for death. Conceptualization is needed but it should always be for praxis. The thing that *makes* the Kairos Document is that some theologians got together and said, "Come now, let's put these actions into theological conceptuality." This conceptuality isn't really what makes the document, however. What makes the Kairos Document powerful is what the people are doing out there on the field. Somebody had to ask: "What are the people doing?" Conceptualization provides the answers.

May we continue to be prophetic in the life of actions and concepts to the glory of God.

15

Jacquelyn Grant

*"... prophecy will announce the hopeful good news
of future liberation, justice, and peace..."*

— KAIROS DOCUMENT, 4.1

In an Episcopal journal I read a story written by a black woman about the relationship between racism and sexism.

The story, taken from African folklore, goes like this: There was a little boy in an African village who customarily came home from the mission school with excitement about his learnings of the day. On one particular day, he came home with a look of puzzlement on his face. And when he came into his house his father inquired about his puzzlement. The little boy said, "Father, I don't understand this. I go to school every day and the teacher often tells us the story about this lion who they say is the king of the jungle. But this ferocious and strong beast always seems to get killed by the hunter in the story. I don't understand it. If the lion is so strong why does the hunter always kill the lion?" The father responded, "Well, son, until lions learn how to write books, that's the way the story will always end."

Until oppressed people begin to do their own theology, oppressors will always appear to win. The people of South and southern Africa have analyzed apartheid theologically and then have spoken via the Kairos Document.

I think we can get a capsule view of the significance of this document by looking at its message and its mission. For us as a people of God, the message is that people made in God's image as

Jacquelyn Grant is Assistant Professor of Systematic Theology at the Interdenominational Theological Center, Atlanta.

human beings have a right to basic human dignity and liberation. There are basic human rights, principles that come simply with being children of God. The document identifies apartheid and declares it a sin. It is heresy; it is illegitimate. The people of South Africa have named apartheid the primary sin and the real heresy in that context. They have called for social, political, and economic transformation that comes by way of revolution of some sort. This is necessary for the integrity of Christianity.

One of the many significant aspects of the document for me is that it relocated and redefined such traditional terms as "reconciliation" and "love," those concepts that are such favorites of oppressors. But the document redefines those terms in such a fashion that they become tools for liberation rather than tools of oppression as they have historically been used.

The document points to the nature of a prophetic church. A prophetic church has several functions:

1. The prophetic church must discern the will of God. Theology as a function of this church is critical. Liberation theology, which is the perspective I have chosen, unequivocally perceives God as being on the side of the oppressed and liberation as being the primary concern of the church. Intrinsic to God's will is the elimination of oppression and injustice and evil wherever they may occur — in South Africa, in southern Africa, or beyond southern Africa.

2. The prophetic church simultaneously exposes the oppressive nature of the society. It goes further to create an agenda of action for liberation of our peoples. The church must stand for liberation and justice even when everyone else is against them.

3. The prophetic church serves as an agent of admonition. It admonishes the people of their wrongdoings, while impressing upon them the need for change to make their actions consistent with God's will. It warns of the consequences of continued disharmony with divine intentions.

4. The prophetic church must move beyond admonition to confrontation of oppression and injustice. Evil must be confronted with the knowledge of divine will as revealed in history.

5. Finally, the prophetic church must create a community of faith, fellowship, peace, justice, and unity. It is incumbent upon this prophetic church to strategize and to employ effective means to insure that these functions are carried out. The Kairos Document prophetically affirms these functions of the church and indeed of anyone engaged in doing theology.

The document points us to a mission. The question for us is, What is our mission in light of the message? I submit that our mission here ought not be to evaluate critically what these South African theologians have done. Our task is to evaluate critically what we are doing. Our task is not to use the Barmen declaration to validate or to justify the Kairos Document. Our task is not even to impose strategies of the black liberation movement upon black South Africans.

The challenge for us is to remember that we must not only look at South Africa, but we must look at ourselves: what are we doing, what must we do? I used to get very frustrated and very irritated with white liberals, a lot of whom were my friends, who would ask, "What can we do about the race question, what can we do?" My response would always be, "You know what you need to do. Racism exists and it needs to be eliminated. You know what you must do." I used to become equally frustrated with my liberal male friends who in dealing with the sexism question would always ask, "What can we do?" And I would always respond, "You know what you must do."

The reason for my frustration is that in the question "what can I do" there is implied the more specific question, "what can I do in your community — the community of the oppressed?" I think that we as North Americans know what we must do. And I think if the Kairos Document does anything for us it ought to inspire us; it ought to force us in the direction of self-examination and self-criticism, that is, we must examine and evaluate our own reality. It ought to force us in the direction of seeing how it is that our lifestyles undergird and therefore perpetuate the oppressed lifestyles of others across the world.

The document ends on a message of hope. That was very strategic for me and important for black Americans who know what it means to hope even when it appears there is no reason to hope. This uplifting ending was significant not because it softened the radicality of the statement, because the statement was just as radical even with the message of hope. It was significant because it represented the fact that a people — a black people who have historically been dehumanized, who have been reduced, who have been oppressed — still have that vision, the vision that this indeed is not the kingdom of God, but the kingdom is still to come. This vision of hope is expressed quite pointedly by Maya Angelou. She was writing about black women's experience in her poem, *And Still I Rise.* And the poem concludes like this:

> Out of the huts of history's shame I rise,
> up from the past that's rooted in pain I rise.
> I'm a black ocean leaping and wide,
> welling and swelling,
> I bear in the tides.
> Leaving behind nights of terror and fear, I rise,
> into a daybreak that's wondrously clear, I rise.
> Bringing the gifts that my ancestors gave,
> I am the dream and the hope of [an African people].
> I rise, I rise, I rise.

Indeed South Africa shall rise.

16

Bible Study
by Thomas Hoyt, Jr.

*"Jesus... stood up in the synagogue at Nazareth
to announce his mission... "*

— KAIROS DOCUMENT, 4.5

[16] And he came to Nazareth, where he had been brought up; and he went to the synagogue, as his custom was, on the sabbath day. And he stood up to read;

[17] and there was given to him the book of the prophet Isaiah. He opened the book and found the place where it was written,

[18] "The Spirit of the Lord is upon me, because he has anointed me to preach good news to the poor. He has sent me to proclaim release to the captives and recovering of sight to the blind, to set at liberty those who are oppressed,

[19] to proclaim the acceptable year of the Lord."

[20] And he closed the book, and gave it back to the attendant, and sat down; and the eyes of all in the synagogue were fixed on him.

[21] And he began to say to them, "Today this scripture has been fulfilled in your hearing."

[22] And all spoke well of him and wondered at the gracious words which proceeded out of his mouth; and they said, "Is not this Joseph's son?"

[23] And he said to them, "Doubtless you will quote to me this proverb, 'Physician, heal yourself; what we have heard you did at Capernaum, do here also in your own country.'"

[24] And he said, "Truly I say to you, no prophet is acceptable in his own country.

[25] But in truth, I tell you, there were many widows in Israel in

135

the days of Elijah, when the heaven was shut up three years and six months, when there came a great famine over all the land;

[26] and Elijah was sent to none of them but only to Zarephath, in the land of Sidon, to a woman who was a widow.

[27] And there were many lepers in Israel in the time of the prophet Elisha; and none of them was cleansed, but only Naaman the Syrian."

[28] When they heard this, all in the synagogue were filled with wrath.

[29] And they rose up and put him out of the city, and led him to the brow of the hill on which their city was built, that they might throw him down headlong.

[30] But passing through the midst of them he went away.

[Luke 4:16–30 RSV]

The Kairos Document proposes a Prophetic Theology as that most appropriate for the situation in South Africa. In doing so it invokes the prophetic tradition of the Hebrew scriptures and the prophetic ministry of Jesus. Here we shall consider the "programmatic" text of Luke 4:16–30, where Jesus inaugurates his prophetic ministry.

Luke 4:16–30 has been called the entire Gospel in a nutshell. It is the prelude to all that will come after. Robert C. Tannehill describes the event at Nazareth as having "typical and programmatic significance for the whole of Jesus' ministry as Luke understands it."[1] The introduction of themes that recur elsewhere in Luke-Acts is a major indication of the programmatic nature of the passage.

The importance of this text is further shown by the manner in which Luke borrowed the original story from Mark and determined its form and position within his Gospel to create his original version. Many scholars maintain that while verses 25–27 have come to Luke from one tradition and verse 23 has been incorporated from another source (with its mention of Capernaum and the proverb), Luke has constructed the scene at Nazareth by rewriting the Markan account. Verses 17–21 and 28–30 are probably from Luke's own pen.[2] In the words of Tannehill, "the most convincing view of the origin of this pericope is that Luke has rewritten the Markan account, supplementing it with fragments of tradition and with material of his own composition."[3]

Regardless of one's opinion concerning the origin of Luke's account, one thing is clear: the point of the Lukan passage is no longer simply the rejection at Nazareth; it has been expanded to introduce what Jesus' ministry is all about. This passage is Jesus' kerygmatic announcement, substituted for Mark 1:14b–15, which Luke omits.

The Inaugural Sermon

As Luke's plan develops, the sequence seems to be deliberate, as seen in the cry of John the Baptist, the baptism of Jesus, the establishment of Jesus' divine and human ancestry, aborted attempts of "Satan" to impede the divine plan of salvation, and Jesus' travels from Jerusalem to Galilee (4:14a). Jesus has now come to the discovery of who he is and recognizes that the Spirit of God is upon him. His fame spreads throughout the entire region (4:14b), and his teaching is universally acclaimed (4:15). The next step seems obvious: the public announcement of his mission, which takes place in the synagogue at Nazareth (4:16–30).

Jesus, on the Sabbath, went into the synagogue of his hometown of Nazareth. He was following both his own and the Jewish custom (4:16). He stood to read the scripture from the scroll of the prophet Isaiah. He opened the scroll and sought his passage.

The Greek word *heuren* of verse 17 does not mean "he found," but "he sought till he found," a fact many commentators and translators have overlooked. The text that Jesus read, Isaiah 61:1–2, is so central to Jesus' teaching (and to the themes of Luke's Gospel) that it is unacceptable to ascribe its selection to a coincidence. No, when Jesus was handed the Isaian scroll, he deliberately searched for this passage. If we remember that the scroll was probably thirty feet long and that it had to be unwound from the left spindle on to the right one, that Isaiah 61:1–2b is almost at the end of the book, and that in Jesus' time the text had not been subdivided into chapters, verses, or paragraphs, we may well imagine that it took Jesus some minutes before he located the text he wanted. If indeed Jesus delivered this sermon, one does not wonder that Luke remarks: "All eyes in the synagogue were fixed on him"! Luke (or Jesus) wanted this text and no other, because in his search of the scriptures he had identified this text as central.

Essentially, verses 18 and 19 are a loose quotation of Isaiah 61:1, 2a (LXX) and an additional clause from Isaiah 58:6. Since Luke probably had a fondness for the Septuagint (the Greek translation), we would expect a great deal of agreement with it. Luke

4:18–19 follows closely the Septuagint, including its word order and its variations from the Hebrew text; nevertheless, there are some significant differences between the Septuagint and the Lukan version of Isaiah.

Luke substitutes "proclaim" for "call" in two instances in verse 19. After "he has sent me," Luke omits "to heal those who have been brokenhearted." Luke adds a phrase from Isaiah 58:6, "to set at liberty those who are oppressed."[4] Finally, the quotation ends abruptly in the midst of Isaiah 61:2 and omits the phrase "and the day of vengeance." The omission of this phrase from Luke implies that Jesus spoke words of mercy and grace, which probably accounts for the reaction of the Jews to Jesus' words, and which might even have prompted John to inquire of Jesus' identity (7:19–23).

The differences between the Lukan version and the texts from which he quotes may be the result of combined or isolated factors. First, the quotation in Luke may have been taken from a tradition of the Septuagint that no longer exists; second, some or all of the variations may be due to an attempt by either Luke or the church to recall the Old Testament passages from memory; or third, the quotation may reflect editorializing. A closer look at these Septuagintal changes suggests that Luke 4:18–19 is an interpretive rendering of the Isaianic passages designed to emphasize a particular point. Otherwise, how do we explain how Jesus, while reading, or Luke while composing, could omit two particular phrases? Even more important, how could he have added a phrase (58:6) that was not even in the text that he is purported to have read? Apparently, the quotation merely helps us see that church tradition early depicted Jesus' ministry in the light of Isaiah 61:1–2. Whatever the reasons for the variations of the Septuagint, those variations confirm that an interpretation of the use of the quotation must be made in the light of the messianic implications of the passage.[5]

"The Spirit of the Lord is upon me." The opening line of Isaiah touches on a theme of special importance to Luke. In both the Gospel and Acts, the role of the Spirit is crucial. Jesus is conceived by the Spirit, baptized by the Spirit, empowered by the Spirit, the bearer of the Spirit, anointed by the Spirit, and the entire story of the church in Acts is a continuation of the work of the Spirit.

Not only in this episode, but throughout the Gospel, Luke

points out the effect of the Spirit on the people when Jesus is present. The people are astonished, filled with awe, and obedient to his commands as they see signs of the inbreaking of the kingdom and the Spirit's manifestation.

The Greek word for "poor" in 4:18 is *ptochos.* The Hebrew word that lay behind the Greek of Isaiah 61:1 is *anawim.* This latter word usually means pious, God-fearing folk. Probably the word as used in 4:18 has religious significance. Manson postulates that "poor," as well as "captives," "blind," and "oppressed," meant victims of inward repressions and spiritual ills. Hence, Jesus was offering spiritual deliverance.[6] This observation appears to be only partially correct. It minimizes both the historical occasion and the Lukan context of the text.

The nature of Isaiah 61:1 must be remembered in any interpretation of 4:18–19. Gilmour says, "The original expressed some post-exilic prophet's consciousness of mission."[7] The mission was to herald a joyous return from Babylonian exile, with the imagery of the year of Jubilee saturating the whole. The phrase "to proclaim the acceptable year of the Lord" (4:19) suggests the imagery of the Old Testament's year of Jubilee. The year of Jubilee included the following four prescriptions: (1) leaving soil fallow, (2) the remission of debts, (3) the liberation of slaves, (4) the return of family property to each individual.

Paul Hollenbach offers a striking summary of this Sabbath-Jubilee tradition in other Torah texts: There are to be no poor, i.e., disinherited, in Israel according to its covenant with Yahweh; however, if Israel breaks the covenant and Israelites wrong (i.e., dishonor) each other and Yahweh, and poor appear, their needs are to met generously: their immediate need for food and clothing, their short-term need for family restoration, and their long-term need for total social reconstruction; in these ways the honor of the disinherited and of Yahweh will be restored.[8]

After this summary, Hollenbach sets up a schema for understanding the thinking and deeds of Jesus that stems directly from the Sabbath-Jubilee tradition. He says:

> The purpose of SJ (Sabbath-Jubilee) provisions is to prevent the permanent degradation of the poor by meeting their needs in these three time frames and in two social settings. Meeting needs in immediate, short-term, and long-term frames we

may call care, redemption, and release. The social settings
are kinship and politics. The first two time frames concern
the kin of those in need, while the third concerns the total
community. This is so because the first two kinds of need are
largely individual, while the third is a matter of the structure
of the whole society. The first two needs can be met by
philanthropic acts, while the third can be met only through
a reordering of the whole social structure. The first two are
designed to prevent the need for the third, but the third is
necessary because the first two don't do the job. In short,
the SJ legislation is designed to prevent the development of
an aristocratic-peasant society out of a covenantal egalitarian
society, but should such a shift occur, the legislation also is
designed to prevent its being permanently established.[9]

In the conversation with John's disciples, Jesus makes known the
nature of his ministry, which was in doubt by John. "Are you the
one who is to come, or shall we look for another?" The several tasks
to be carried out by the one anointed by the Spirit are suggested
in Luke 7:21–22 as presently being carried out in the ministry of
Jesus.

In that hour he cured many of diseases and plagues and evil
spirits, and on many that were blind he bestowed sight. And
he answered them, "Go and tell John what you have seen and
heard: the blind receive their sight, the lame walk, lepers are
cleansed, and the deaf hear, the dead are raised up, the poor
have good news preached to them."

This quotation fits perfectly the theme of the opening sermon of
Jesus. What could it mean that the "blind receive their sight?"
Allan Boesak of South Africa has some wonderful images of what
these phrases in Luke really mean:

What else can it mean but that people can now see themselves
as God sees them. They can see their human possibilities as
well as they see their present situation. They can see a future
of freedom and human dignity to which they have been blind
before.

The lame walk:

What could it mean for those who for so long were lying by the wayside crippled by feelings of inferiority, fear and lack of vision?

Boesak says of his poor and oppressed fellow pilgrims:

> We got so used to our lowly position, we accepted our suffering as God's will. We stared ourselves blind against the white man's power and his guns. We were lame! Jesus is saying to us: the kingdom is yours! Get up and walk. Its power is yours: stand up and be strong.

Lepers are cleansed:

> God has touched the poor in Jesus the Messiah. God has given untouchables a new self-image of worthfulness.

The deaf hear. What do they hear?

> They hear good news. No longer a pseudo-gospel designed to justify oppression and comfort for the oppressor. No longer a gospel so spiritualized that it has become anemic and incapable of dealing with the harsh realities, . . . but a word of liberation and freedom and human dignity.[10]

The dead are raised up: There are various kinds of death. There is physical death; there is death that one experiences outside the human community. This latter experience is the death of a person who is merely property and is not accepted by others. More importantly, there is a death in which one is not at peace with oneself, when one does not accept oneself as a vital link in the human community.

To all these people Jesus preaches the good news that God in Messiah Jesus has seen the condition of the people, has taken upon God's self the condition of the people, and taken their cause as God's own. That is the good news: God will fill the hungry with good things and the rich God will send away empty (Luke 1:53). The Sovereign One works vindication and justice for all who are oppressed (Ps. 103:6). The good news is that the Sovereign One is here to execute justice for the oppressed, to give food to the hungry, to uphold the widow and the fatherless, and to bring to ruin the way of the wicked.

Rejection at Home

This announcement of a new age in 4:18–19 contained an inherent criticism of all those powers and agents of the present order. We are surprised, therefore, by the initial reaction of the crowd: "They wondered at the gracious words which proceeded out of his mouth" (v. 22). The record of Matthew 13:57 and Mark 6:3 states that the crowd took offense at him. The initial reaction of the crowd in Luke later turned into the same reaction.

The final rejection by the crowd ensued because Jesus continued to talk about prophets lacking honor in their own country (v. 24). He also recounted in a second sermon (vv. 25–28) the Old Testament stories of Elijah and Elisha. These two prophets in their ministry to Gentiles were used to illustrate the proverb: "No prophet is accepted in his own country" (v. 24). Both prophets were more successful with Gentiles (strangers) than with Jews. Elijah ministered to the widow at Zarephath, a Sidonian town, and Elisha healed Namaan, a leper in Syria.

The implications are twofold: (1) Those of Jesus' territory will not understand, and the Gentiles will. Luke once again stresses universalism. (2) Jesus' way of salvation did not sustain the idea of preference, which some of the Jews had derived from their belief in God's election of them. God's love and redemption were for all. God was free to love and choose whomever God desired. "The acceptable year of the Lord" was for all people.

The hometown folk rejected Jesus because they refused to believe that the village boy, the son of a carpenter, whom they had known from infancy, had a right to talk with them as a prophet. The crowd became incensed and wanted to cast him out of their village. They held his background against him, but, more importantly, their pride and prejudice stood in the way of their acceptance of his message and the universality of the good news that God had visited God's people.

Jesus' deed and the word have combined to give power to the proclamation on behalf of the poor. There is release for the captives, sight for the blind, and liberty for the oppressed. In the words of the Kairos Document,

> God is not neutral.... "God, who does what is right, is always on the side of the oppressed" (Ps. 103:6).... Jesus, the Son

of God, also takes up the cause of the poor and the oppressed and identifies himself with their interests.... God is at work in our world turning hopeless and evil situations to good so that God's Kingdom may come and God's Will may be done on earth as it is in heaven. (4.5)

Notes

1. Robert C. Tannehill, "The Mission of Jesus According to Luke 4:16–30," in Walther Elthester, ed., *Jesus in Nazareth* (Berlin: deGruyter, 1972), p. 51.

2. Joseph Fitzmyer, *Luke,* Anchor Bible (New York: Doubleday, 1981), pp. 526–527. See also Walter E. Pilgrim, *Good News to the Poor: Wealth and Poverty in Luke-Acts* (Minneapolis: Augsburg, 1981), p. 64; Howard Marshall, *The Gospel of Luke: A Commentary on the Greek Text.* (Grand Rapids: Eerdmans, 1978), p. 178.

3. Tannehill, "The Mission of Jesus," p. 52.

4. G.W. Lampe, "Luke," in *Peake's Commentary on the Bible,* ed. M. Black, rev. ed. (London: Thomas Nelson and Sons, 1962), p. 828, stipulates that the clause added from Isa. 58:6 enables Luke "to introduce his favorite theme of 'release,' a word generally used in the sense of 'forgiveness' (of sins), which for him is the essence of the gospel."

5. Cf. James Muilenburg, *The Book of Isaiah, Chapters 40–66: Introduction and Exegesis,* Interpreter's Bible, 5:708–709. He sees that the Isaianic passages are descriptive of the anticipated mission of the Servant of Yahweh during the Messianic era.

6. William Manson, *The Gospel of Luke* (New York: R.R. Smith, 1930), pp. 41–42.

7. S.M. Gilmour, *The Gospel According to St. Luke,* Interpreter's Bible (1952), 8:91.

8. See Paul Hollenbach, "Liberating Jesus for Social Involvement," *Biblical Theology Bulletin,* vol. 15, p. 153.

9. Ibid.

10. Allan Boesak, "Shall We look For Another?" *The Reformed Journal,* vol. 31 (June 1981), p. 19.

Part Five
THE KAIROS COVENANT

17

The Kairos Covenant

"... we would also like to repeat our call
to our Christian brothers and sisters
throughout the world ... "

— KAIROS DOCUMENT, Conclusion

An Initial Response of U.S. Christians
in Solidarity with the Oppressed in South Africa

This is a time of crisis and judgment, a *kairos* for U.S. Christians. God speaks to us today. In the prophetic cry of our sisters and brothers in South Africa we hear God's Word.

- It is a call for confession and repentance for our participation in the sin of apartheid;

- It is a call to conversion, and we give thanks for it;

- It is a call to speak out and take action against the fears, the rationalizations, the paralysis, the policies, the structures — whether in church or society, whether in the U.S., South Africa, or elsewhere in the world — against all that contributes to continue oppression.

The grace of God compels us to respond.

The *kairos* of these times judges our nation as well. U.S. administration support of the government of South Africa is mirrored by a domestic policy, grounded in racism, that imposes economic apartheid. Its victims are disproportionately men, women, and

This document was prepared by the participants in the Kairos Covenant convocation, Chicago, November 1986.

children of color. The majority of our people remain insensitive to the poverty and oppression, unaware of our complicity in the systems that inflict and prolong the suffering.

Called to a new radical commitment by the *kairos* of our times and in active solidarity with our oppressed sisters and brothers in South Africa, we pledge in the name of Jesus Christ, crucified and resurrected:

- to tell the truth about the evil of apartheid in South Africa and work to abolish it;

- to offer increased support to the people of South Africa in their own struggle;

- to support the peoples of southern Africa who are victims of U.S. and South African political, military, and economic destabilization;

- to speak the truth of justice in our churches;

- to fight racism, sexism, and economic injustice in our own society;

- to challenge our social and political structures to send clear messages to the South African government: we will not as a nation tolerate apartheid, and we will encourage all other nations to stand together against it;

- to renounce a self-centered U.S. lifestyle that exists at the expense of blacks in South Africa and other oppressed people in our country and throughout the world.

The hour is late. The judgment of God is at hand. God asks us to love more deeply, work more diligently, risk more courageously. We give thanks to God for this opportunity to help prepare the way for the gift of a reign of justice in which the present signs of death will be swept away and God's new life will fill us all.

The Rev. Don Prange
Hope Daria
Richard Mouw
Audrey Sorrento
Robert McAfee Brown
Eva Jensen
Maurice Ngakane

Edward Schroeder
Herman Diers
William E. Palmer
Rev. Al Sampson
Randolph Harlan Miller
Thomas R. McGowan
Nathaniel Garry Grai

Rev. Willie Goodman, Jr.

Harry W. Cooper, Jr.

Sister Joanette Nitz, O.P.

Sister Jamie T. Phelps, O.P.

Josiah Young

Sister M. Shawn Copeland, O.P.

James E. Hug, S.J.

Eugene Blocker

Joseph Thompson

Susan Burchfield

Brian Burchfield

Julius S. Nelson, Jr.

J. Robert Hur

Erna Kiesaling

MacGaffrey

A. E. Hope

Dorothea Hudert

Juliana Mislovic

Sybela Thomas

Janet L. Kuttlaus

Randall N. Lohn

Wm. Petterson

Elkin Sithole

Stanley W. Green

Hlenfr Uklyl

Wilma Jakobsen

Willis Logan

Josephine Lucker

Gabriel M. Setiloane

Nnako P. Moila

David Mesenbring

Kim Rue

Sue Hartsell

Gloria Hannas

Marion Hughes

Prudence Angela Robinson

Marie J. Giblin, M.M.

Abraham Akrong

E. Branson

Maxine M. Washington

Lois Kirkwood

Porter Kirkwood

Dwight A. Hopkins

Angela Hardy

Audrey Glover

Janet C. Palrud

David Bower

Wes Albin

Marie J. King

David M. Whitermore

Cherie L. Deck

Thomas Malnit

Angela L. Battle

Ike M. Grenhze

Lisa E. Dahill

Scott Asseng

Paul D. Tierhson

Paula V. Michel

Dr. Albert Pero

Meredith Lloyd

Joe Seoka

M. P. Moila

Burgess Carr

B. Z. Mkantane

Pauline Odita

18

Harold Washington

"... it is a matter of what type of sanctions to apply..."
— KAIROS DOCUMENT, Preface, rev. ed.

The suffering people of South Africa impel a response, even force a response from those who are on record time and time again as to where they stand. We must constantly raise our voices against what is happening there. In the process of doing so, often times we should draw parallels between there and here; sometimes the two are not so far apart.

We in Chicago have heeded the call from within South Africa and calls from leaders like Bishop Tutu. Bishop Tutu was in Chicago and lifted the whole spiritual and moral level and tone of this city for at least twenty-four hours. I had hoped that that would last much longer. Perhaps if he came back at least once a month we would sustain ourselves another 150 years. Also Rev. Allan Boesak and Rev. Beyers Naude and organizations like the South Africa Council of Churches (SACC) and the Congress of South Africa Trade Unions all have called for disinvestment and withdrawals.

The City of Chicago, in June of 1986, adopted disinvestment measures applicable to its own funds and its own purchases. We went as far as the law would permit us to go — not far enough clearly. But it was at least one more voice among other voices being constantly raised in opposition to what we see in that country.

Chicago is in the ranks of the nineteen states, thirteen counties, and seventy cities that have taken actions to keep city funds from being connected to South Africa or U.S. companies and banks

Harold Washington was mayor of Chicago until his death in November 1987.

involved with South Africa and its apartheid system. We must do more especially regarding the giant holdings of public pension funds. We have to raise the level of public discussion, raise the level of criticism, continue to point the finger, continue to make people completely and totally uncomfortable in their never-ending quest to grab the almighty dollar with no concern for what it does to their morality or to the lives of people. We call on the legislature to pass disinvestment laws.

I support legislation to prohibit further investment of Illinois State pension funds in South Africa. Illinois legislators should have been able to make it clear where they stood on the issue. They didn't do that. A glorious chance was lost to have serious public discussion and perhaps get the State of Illinois to speak very loudly on apartheid in South Africa.

We have work to do. We have to reflect deeply on apartheid. Let us be fruitful and multiply those we can convince to take their stand with us.

Along the long trail of history, a person sometimes stands and says, "Enough!" It might as well be now.

19

Sing Sing Statement

"The challenge... of our present kairos
is addressed to all who bear the name Christian... "

— KAIROS DOCUMENT, Concl.

We, students of the New York Theological Seminary program at Sing Sing Correctional Facility, Ossining, New York, have come together from various prisons across New York state to earn our Masters degrees in Professional Studies.

From September 3, 1985, to June 28, 1986, we have met together to study theology and the many ways that God has interacted with humankind. We have committed ourselves to the discovery of God's presence within our prison experience and to an in-depth biblical reading of the signs of the times. We believe that the Word of God can be read in the liberating events of peoples' lives.

We have come together also to reflect upon the oppression of blacks by whites in South Africa. The focus of our reflection has been the Kairos Document: "Challenge to the Church: A Theological Comment on the Political Crisis in South Africa."

Together the eleven of us have experienced over 115 years of incarceration, and as a result of our experience, observations, and ministry, we can testify to the suffering, agony, and servitude of those incarcerated in the New York prison system.

We see parallels between our lives in prison and the lives of those who live under the system of apartheid. And we can point to the similar captivity of the children of Israel who lived in bondage

This statement was prepared by theology students at Sing Sing Correctional Facility, Ossining, New York.

in Egypt: "Their cry went up to God, who heard their groaning..." (Exod. 2:23–24).

We feel a special empathy for those incarcerated by the South
African government, including many children and young people
whose most basic human rights are denied.

Taken as a whole, the Bible authorizes Christians to resist repressive governments (notwithstanding the use sometimes made of
Romans 13 and other passages taken out of context). The Old
Testament is clearly a testimony that God actively supports the
removal of repressive governments: "I will make your oppressors
kill each other; they will be drunk with murder and rage" (Isa.
49:26; cf. Jer. 30:18–24).

We believe that Christians who condemn apartheid as "ungodly" without actively seeking its destruction are themselves ungodly: "What good is it for someone to say he has faith if his
actions do not prove it?" (James 2:14).

We have a mandate to fight the influences of Satan, and to
accomplish this we support massive, non-violent direct action. But
we must not be quick to condemn the use of violence by the South
African people in their efforts to overcome the devilish government
forces there. We celebrate the martyrdom of those who have died
in this struggle.

Remembering that God is an active God and that Jesus led
an active ministry (see Luke 4:18–19; Isa. 61:1–2), we believe that
the churches must be active in their opposition to apartheid. We
believe the churches must mobilize their resources to assist in the
overthrow of the repressive South African government. At the same
time we recognize the role of many others, who are not Christian,
in this struggle.

We have endeavored to formulate a number of proposals in
response to the Kairos Document:

- We call for majority rule in South Africa, so that reconciliation and holistic growth can begin — growth of spirit, soul,
  and body (see 1 Thess. 5:23).

- We call for a total transformation of the oppressive practices
  of the South African government; the changes must be structural, for individual conversions are not enough. We call on
  the South African government to restore the land to its original owners.

- We call on the churches inside and outside South Africa to expose the hypocrisy of those who claim to be Christians while siding with the oppressors of South Africa. For example, the Vatican bank, the Instituto per le Opere de Religione (IOR), has been financing South African apartheid through its subsidiaries.

- We call on the churches to emphasize the need for all who are oppressed to participate in the liberation struggle of South Africans, with the church itself serving as a role model.

- We call on Christians in South Africa to dissociate themselves from any church that supports apartheid, for the authority of the church cannot supersede the Word of God, and God is always on the side of the oppressed.

- We call on the churches to break the ideological power of the oppressors, exercised through the control of symbols. The oppressed must not be subjugated by the language of their oppressors, but instead educate themselves in the language of the prophetic and apocalyptic traditions.

- We call on Christians throughout the world to encourage and support any and all strikes by the oppressed within South Africa.

- We call on the churches throughout the world to petition their governments to condemn apartheid and to impose appropriate economic sanctions. We call for the boycott of the sale of all gold products from South Africa; any gold product that does not expressly state its country of origin should be assumed to be South African. Christians should boycott and picket any manufacturer or retailer, large or small, who buys or sells any product made in South Africa. Whether a can of sardines or a diamond ring, if it comes from South Africa it should not be bought or sold. Pastors must inform their congregations of these sanctions in their sermons and in informal conversations.

- We call on South African Christian to disregard accusations that they are Marxist or Communist, simply because they oppose the oppressive status quo.

- We call upon the churches in the United States to set aside one day a week on which Christians will abstain from spending any money for anything. This will pressure our government to participate more actively in the overthrow of the South African government. We feel that black Christians have a special obligation to support such a boycott.

- We call on the churches inside and outside South Africa to oppose cultural exchanges between South Africa and the international community of artists and writers, dancers and musicians.

- We call on the churches to organize fundraising activities to provide aid for the people of South Africa as they resist oppression through strikes, boycotts, demonstrations, etc. With independent sources of income, these brothers and sisters need not be dependent upon the society that is the source of their oppression.

We express our solidarity with the South African symbol of freedom. Nelson Mandela, and with the other freedom fighters incarcerated or in exile.

The *kairos* is at hand. Let us not be like the hypocrites condemned by Jesus: "You can look at the earth and the sky and predict the weather; why, then, don't you know the meaning of the present time?" (Luke 12:56).

George Franklin	*Julio Cesar Maldonado*
Charles Frazier	*Roy Melvin*
Morris Howard	*Herbert Payne*
Donald Jones	*Robert Dawad Smith*
Angel Rosado Maldonado	*Robert Turner*

Leon O. Woods

Part Six
DISCUSSION GUIDE

by David Mesenbring

Introduction

On September 13, 1985, over 150 Christians from more than twenty denominations in South Africa published their "Challenge to the Church: A Theological Comment on the Political Crisis in South Africa." It is a statement that has evolved from discussion at a grassroots level by lay and clergy throughout the local communities and churches of South Africa. Since its release, thousands of South African Christians have added their signatures to this statement of theology that has become known as the "Kairos Document." Keeping its self-stated promise to further evolve through continuing discussion, a second, revised edition of the Kairos Document, with more biblical references, was published in South Africa one year after the first edition.

Christians in different parts of the world are studying the Kairos Document in order to identify with persecuted Christians in southern Africa. No ecumenical statement of theology has received such wide attention since individual German Christians signed the Barmen Declaration during World War II challenging the heresy of Nazism. The reasons are due both to the authenticity with which the document engages the southern Africa context as well as the Kairos Document's relevance to the situation of Christians in North America and western Europe. The Kairos Document has become well-known for its prophetic denunciation of injustice and its urgent call to actively resist evil.

Publication of the Kairos Document coincided with an escalation of apartheid's violence that has thrust South Africa into the eye of the Western media. Such coverage has popularized the study of South Africa by Western Christians whose interests often mirror, rather than model, interest of the society-at-large. However, Christians who study the Kairos Document are discovering that the church in South Africa offers a theological challenge more

David Mesenbring is a free-lance consultant on southern African issues serving North American churches. Three of his last eleven years were spent inside South Africa working with churches there. A preliminary version of this study design was tested among various lay, clergy, and university groups of Lutherans in the Pacific Northwest. The author is grateful for their generous cooperation and the suggested design changes that resulted from those discussions. This discussion guide was originally published by the Theology in Global Context Program, 475 Riverside Drive, New York, NY 10115; it has been edited for this volume and is included here with permission.

profound than secularized Westerners have been expecting. The very surprise of this discovery can lead to new awareness about the presence of racism in the midst of our own lives.

Some say that God gave individuals limitations so that they would have to cooperate in community. The Xhosa people of South Africa express this with their proverb *"umntu ngumntu ngabantu,"* which means "a person is a person because of other people." But perhaps the Akun people of Ghana say it best with their proverb *"adwen wotua tua,"* which translates as "wisdom is pieced together from the insights of several persons." This proverb is used to counter people who think that they have a monopoly on wisdom and truth. Study of the Kairos Document illustrates the truth of these proverbs by providing Christians everywhere with access to other people's theological insights.

Christian theology helps people to transcend their own narrow interests and to look to the interests of the common good. South Africans have already learned a lot of theology from North Americans; now it is time that we listen to — and learn from — them. This is especially urgent at a time when the violence of their situation is escalating so rapidly. But it is also fraught with difficulty since the very people we want to identify with have long accused us of profiting from their exploitation. In short, we must be honest about the fact that it is not in our (narrowly defined) "economic interest" to help bring fundamental changes to southern Africa. Only by the grace of God can we hope to transcend our self-interests in favor of the larger good. In this sense, the access that black South African Christians offer us to a larger point of view can be understood as God's grace; the Church Universal (mostly poor) is one of God's gifts of undeserved grace to North American Christians (who are relatively rich).

A discussion guide for groups that want to spend five sessions studying the Kairos Document is included here. Its purpose is to foster a fresh encounter with the Word of God. Discussion participants can hope to gain new understanding about familiar Bible passages and tenets of theology. This is because they will be discussing the theology and faith of Christians whose life experience is very different from that of most North Americans. Participants will not simply learn more about the situation in southern Africa, but be challenged by the challenging faith of South African Christians.

The discussion guide emphasizes a New Testament call to unity. Just as the Kairos Document was written in an ecumenical context, so also will those who study and reflect on it need to pray for new ecumenical commitment if they are to renew their Christian faith through this encounter with a long overlooked member of the Body of Christ. Discussion participants should not measure the Kairos Document's theological "correctness" against the doctrine of any single denomination. It was born of ecumenical impetus and can inspire ecumenical community among those with "ears to hear." The Word of God has remained dynamic through the centuries precisely because it continues to profoundly address new situations. Since black South Africans today face a reality quite different from that which is familiar to North Americans, it should surprise no one that their reading of the Bible will bear unique emphases.

Purposes

- Expose North American Christians to some themes of popular South African theology.

- Facilitate an encounter in which North American theology becomes enriched by South African perspectives.

- Stimulate critical self-reflection by North Americans about factors biasing their relations with oppressed people in southern Africa.

General Notes to the Discussion Leader

1. The discussion outline that follows does not presume advance reading of the document. You are strongly urged to make copies of the Kairos Document available to each discussion participant and should not be surprised if some do not actually read it until after your discussion series is completed. The Kairos Document is included in Part I of this volume. It may be photocopied in whole or in part. The document may also be purchased in booklet form for $2.95 from Wm. B. Eerdmans Publishing Company, 255 Jefferson Ave. S.E., Grand Rapids, MI 49503 (800/633-9326 or 616/459-4591), or the Theology in Global Context Program, 475 Riverside Drive, New York, NY 10115 (212/870-2429).

2. The study session is designed for discussion rather than lecture. The sessions work best in groups where (*a*) the leader does not dominate discussion; (*b*) one or two participants do not do most of the talking; and (*c*) group participants are willing to engage verbally in the questions suggested. As leader, you should serve to insure that discussion remains focused on the question at hand. Experience in working with this discussion model suggests that participants often have a variety of set opinions on South Africa that they want to work into the discussion. Leaders should vigilantly strive, however, to keep discussion focused on the questions suggested by the study sessions.

If your discussion group is larger than fifteen persons, break into smaller groups in order to facilitate better discussion. As much as possible, composition of the small groups should remain the same from one session to another. At the point of forming small groups during Study Session II, encourage participants to return to the same groupings that were used during the previous session.

3. The discussion outline is recommended for use during five consecutive one-hour sessions. It is designed to stimulate interest in the Kairos Document and does not claim to illuminate all the "most important" sections of that document. Leaders are encouraged to improve the design.

Groups largely unfamiliar with the apartheid problem will benefit from another, preliminary session that makes use of the excellent media resources available on South Africa and Namibia. Contact your regional church office for videos and films. A good (and widely available) resource is the "Winds of Change" film/video study program on apartheid and the churches, featuring interviews with Archbishop Desmond Tutu and Dr. Allan Boesak. A shorter program that would serve well to introduce study of the Kairos Document is "Torture of a South African Pastor." In addition to being widely available on videotape, both of these programs can be rented in the 16mm film format ($25 each, including shipping) from LWM Media at 800/527-3211 (in Texas, call 214/340-2579). For other film and video resources on southern Africa, contact the Southern Africa Media Center, 630 Natoma Street, San Francisco, CA 94103 (415/621-6196).

4. The final chapter of the Kairos Document is called "Challenge to Action." In formulating a response, your group will want to be in touch with some leading anti-apartheid advocacy agencies.

A list of some of these agencies with which you can work is found at the end of this guide (see below pp. 181–184). Participants should also contact church body offices for similar information. As a "homework suggestion" to be started at least two weeks prior to Session V, it is suggested that members of your group each take responsibility for contacting at least one of the agencies to learn about its work. This way, the whole of your group will be better able to join with others in effectively working for an end to the apartheid system.

5. This discussion guide intends to encounter — not debate — the theology of the Kairos Document. Since the Kairos Document reflects the theology of poor people, it will sometimes appear to challenge the theology of rich Christians. Resistance to such challenge is natural and should be anticipated. But rather than simply allowing such challenge to undermine the process of encounter, you may want to persistently ask, "Wouldn't it be good to hear how the authors would respond to that concern?" This simple question will remind participants that (*a*) the authors are not present to defend themselves, and (*b*) the purpose of this discussion is to become exposed to South African theology rather than to debate all its doctrinal ramifications. Any fair debate would have to involve the authors. Unless they are present to represent themselves, the leader should be prepared to meet and deflect those who consciously or unconsciously undermine the encounter. If these study sessions stimulate the hunger of its participants to witness a fair debate, it will have made an important contribution to the current situation.

FIVE STUDY SESSIONS
Participant Material

Study Session I

1. In order to see what South Africans can teach us about reading the Bible, look at a familiar passage and see how we've used it. Read Romans 13:1–7 and describe a specific experience you remember when reference was made to this text. Reflect on whether the intention of the person who quoted the text was to promote or limit a given activity.

2. Take a few minutes to read section 2.1 of the Kairos Document.

3. What new perspective on this Romans text do you gain from the Kairos Document? What fresh insight does it offer you?

4. Discuss whether Paul's purpose in writing to the Romans was to encourage or discourage a more active relationship with the political authorities.

5. Refer back to the specific situations you named in the first question. How will you constructively apply your new insights about this passage if you find yourself in the same situation again?

Study Session II

1. Describe some specific memories you have of a political leader and his or her use of the label "communist."

2. Take a few minutes to read section 2.3 of the Kairos Document.

3. What new perspective does this text give to your understanding of how a State can misuse the label "communist"? Think about the experiences reported in no. 1 and what you can learn from the Kairos Document about how to respond to situations in which the communist label is used.

4. Discuss steps that should be taken in order to effect true Christian reconciliation between white and black people in southern Africa.

5. Take a few minutes to read section 3.1 of the Kairos Document.

6. What new insights did you gain from the Kairos Document about the nature of Christian reconciliation? Would these insights change any of the opinions stated in your discussion of no. 4?

Study Session III

1. Most North Americans form their images and their ideas about South Africa from the major print, radio, and television media. List all the images that come to mind when you hear the phrase "violence in South Africa." Now make another list of images prompted by the phrase "self-defense of South Africans." Try not to think too much about it; simply name the images that first come to mind. Save these lists for later reference.

2. Read section 3.3 of the Kairos Document.

3. Share with each other any new insights gained from reading this material. What is new for you about the way in which these themes are treated by the Kairos Document?

4. Return to the lists of images made in no. 1. How do you think the authors of the Kairos Document would describe the biases reflected in these lists? Which side of the struggle in South Africa would they say that the items on these lists reflect? What kind of balance does our media give us on the "violence" theme? Do we get a different kind of balance with regard to the "self-defense" theme?

5. In 1985 and again in 1986, the South African government declared a national state of emergency that imposed dramatic new levels of press censorship along with other restrictions. Discuss how such censorship is likely to bias the perspective of those North Americans who rely on the media as their primary source for information about southern Africa.

6. Norwegians are proud of the way they resisted Nazi occupation of their country during World War II. Such resistance included ruthless assassination of Nazi collaborators who were called "Quislings." The French underground also threatened collaborators with deadly violence. U.S. media at that time lauded these tactics as heroic acts of self-defense. With fewer weapons at their disposal, and a larger problem of collaboration, black South Africans have evolved a resistance strategy called "necklacing." While the Western press condemns this as barbaric, black South Africans point out that this strategy has been highly effective in thwarting white efforts to recruit new collaborators. Is necklacing found on your list of associations with the phrase "self-defense of South Africans"? Do you think that black South Africans have more or less reason than the Norwegians and French to fight collaborators?

Study Session IV

1. Recall the history of the American Revolutionary War and the resistance to British colonial rule. Was the violence of American patriots in that situation justified by their struggle against the British? By what factors do you reach your conclusion that such tactics were or were not justified?

2. Read section 4.4 of the Kairos Document.

3. Discuss those points from your reading of section 4.4 that represent new perspectives for you.

4. List the various types of violence required to perpetuate the apartheid system. List both direct and indirect types of violence including any violent effects that result from the continuation of apartheid.

5. Ignore, for a moment, the long history of commitment to non-violence featured in the policies of the African National Congress (ANC) between 1912 and 1960. Today, "armed struggle" is one of many ANC strategies to end apartheid. List the various types of violence currently employed by South Africans trying to overthrow the apartheid regime.

6. In his book *The Riddle of Violence,* Dr. Kenneth Kaunda, President of Zambia, recalls the period of 1965 when a renegade white minority government in Rhodesia declared itself independent from Britain. This unilateral declaration of independence was a means by which white Rhodesians tried to evade British pressure for greater black political rights. At that time, Kaunda urged the British to avert a certain outbreak of civil war by using moderate force to impress upon white Rhodesians the need for change. Britain, claiming to prefer a "non-violent" solution, instead opted for economic sanctions. Kaunda points out that Britain's so-called non-violent policy resulted in fifteen years of civil war that claimed 20,000 lives before blacks finally got the right to vote in what is now Zimbabwe. The South African government and the ANC both claim that their violent tactics are necessary to counter each other's violent posture. Keeping in mind what you have read in section 4.4 of the Kairos Document, which side is God calling you to align yourself with at this *kairos* moment?

Study Session V

   1. Read the Conclusion of the Kairos Document.

   2. Listen to reports from those members of your discussion group who used the homework suggestion to research available action opportunities.

   3. What new relationship with southern Africa will you be motivated to seek as the direct result of studying the Kairos Document?

   4. Has discussion of the Kairos Document had any influence on your theology? If so, what?

   5. What steps, if any, will you take to gain further exposure to the theology of "oppressed Christians"?

Notes for the Leader

Study Session I

Materials needed:

   Photocopies of Participant Material (p. 161 above)
   Bibles
   Copies of the Kairos Document, section 2.1

It is expected that you will have read the Kairos Document in advance, although many other discussion participants may not have. Begin your study by briefly explaining the meaning of the term *kairos* as explained in Chapter One of the Kairos Document (see above p. 7). Then explain that Study Session I will focus on Chapter Two, entitled "Critique of State Theology" (see above pp. 9–15). It may help to point out that the South African State generally receives strong support from the White Dutch Reformed churches of South Africa. These churches are largely attended by Afrikaners, who make up about 60 percent of the white population. Distinction should be made between Afrikaans- and English-speaking South Africans.

As background for this session see Part II above, "State Theology," especially pp. 54–58 of Richard Mouw's contribution and Thomas Hoyt's study, pp. 70–77.

1. *In order to see what South Africans can teach us about reading the Bible, look at a familiar passage and see how we've used it. Read Romans 13:1–7 and describe a specific experience you remember when reference was made to this text. Reflect on whether the intention of the person who quoted the text was to promote or limit a given activity.*

The first discussion question will require the careful engagement of your participants. If people hesitate to recall actual situations in their personal experience, it may help to ask the group whether this passage is, in fact, familiar. When someone says "yes," ask them in what situation they remember it being used. If someone cites a historical instance where this text was used (such as Nazi Germany), remind them that the question asks about the participant's own personal experience. The key is for people to be very specific about citing a concrete experience in their own life history when someone made reference to this text.

This discussion question also asks participants to consider what was intended by the person who quoted Romans 13 in the situation being described. It is expected that most will agree that the usual North American reference to Romans 13 intends to squelch (or at least criticize) some sort of controversial political involvement. For example, if this passage is quoted to someone who has practiced civil disobedience, chances are that the quotation comes from a Christian who does not approve of the political behavior of the one who has disobeyed the law. It is important for your group to discuss whether common North American reference to Romans 13 usually encourages or discourages an active relationship to the political authorities.

2. *Take a few minutes to read section 2.1 of the Kairos Document.*

If not every participant has a copy of the Kairos Document, then be sure to photocopy section 2.1 in advance of the session and distribute copies to each person.

3. *What new perspective on this Romans text do you gain from the Kairos Document? What fresh insight does it offer you?*

Discussion of this point can easily become very wide ranging. It may be necessary to remind the group frequently to share new insights that emerge from reading this particular section of the Kairos Document.

It is hoped that the whole issue of interpreting Scripture "in context" will arise. The "context" referred to by the Kairos Document includes at least two themes: (*a*) the importance of interpreting a particular passage in a manner consistent with the rest of the Bible; and (*b*) understanding the social and historical context of the people to whom Paul was writing. Yet a third kind of context that you may want to draw out of your discussion concerns that context of community within which the Scriptures are read. Consider, for example, the degree to which Romans 13 looks different when read by and with South African Christians. What does this suggest about the importance of broadening the global dimensions of that community within which North American Christians study God's Word? Some groups that have studied the Kairos Document conclude that Scripture is either used to reinforce the values of its readers or to transform them.

4. *Discuss whether Paul's purpose in writing to the Romans was to encourage or discourage a more active relationship with the political authorities.*

The Kairos Document authors interpret Romans 13 as a strong statement encouraging one's conscious relationship to political authorities. Some discussion participants will want to argue that Paul defines this relationship as one of subjection. It may help to bear in mind that the concept of an active citizenship of democratic participation was much less developed then than it is today. Given Paul's strong admonition against the tendency of Christians to dissociate from the government, it may be inferred that if Paul were writing today, he would encourage a relationship with government that is active (as citizens) rather than passive (as subjects).

5. *Refer back to the specific situations you named in the first question. How will you constructively apply your new insights about this passage if you find yourself in the same situation again?*

This discussion item is important for helping participants identify what they have learned from this discussion experience and how they will apply their learning to their life experiences.

Study Session II

Materials needed:
> Photocopies of Participant Material (p. 162 above)
> Copies of the Kairos Document, sections 2.3 and 3.1

This session focuses on Chapters Two and Three of the Kairos Document. Discussion questions 1–3 are concerned with a section from the chapter on "State Theology." Before moving on to question no. 4, you will want to point out that Chapter Three is a critique of "Church Theology" as generally espoused by the leadership of the English-speaking churches. Although largely black in membership, these so-called English-speaking churches are predominantly led and influenced by the 40 percent of South Africa's white population that is English-speaking. There is great rivalry (and some history of bitter struggle) between English- and Afrikaans-speaking white South Africans, so it is not surprising that the Kairos Document should make a distinction between the theologies of these two church traditions.

As background for this session see above Part II, "State Theology," and Part III, "Church Theology," especially the contribution of James Hug, pp. 59–63.

1. *Describe some specific memories you have of a political leader and his or her use of the label "communist."*

Once again, discussion opens by asking participants to call to mind their own (North American) experience of a theme to be discussed. In this case the theme is use of the label "communist" by politicians. Ask participants to cite some experiences they remember when this label was used to identify a person or organization or another government.

2. *Take a few minutes to read section 2.3 of the Kairos Document.*

Since this session will require reading both Kairos Document sections 2.3 and 3.1, you may want to create a photocopy master page that includes both sections on the two sides of one page.

3. *What new perspective does this text give to your understanding of how a State can misuse the label "communist"? Think about the experiences reported in no. 1 and what you can learn from the Kairos Document about responding to situations in which the communist label is used.*

Each time a section of the Kairos Document is read, you are encouraged to let participants simply voice any new insights they have gained from their reading. You can encourage this discussion by asking a series of questions until discussion begins to flow: "What was new for you in reading this material?" "Did you learn anything from reading this?" "What points made a special impression upon you?"

Be careful that your discussion stays focused on what has been learned from reading section 2.3 of the Kairos Document. Some participants may have a tendency to start sharing what they know to be true about the South African situation. But the discussion questions specifically ask what has been learned from reading section 2.3 of the Kairos Document.

The question also asks that people apply any new insights gained from discussing the Kairos Document to their own life situations. It is not necessary for every member of your group to agree with each application suggested by individual members of the group.

4. *Discuss steps that should be taken in order to effect true Christian reconciliation between white and black people in southern Africa.*

This question prepares participants to start focusing on Chapter Three of the Kairos Document. Here, the authors of the Kairos Document will evaluate the way in which church leaders sometimes use the theme of reconciliation. Begin by asking your group to think about how they would apply this theme to the situation in South Africa.

5. *Take a few minutes to read section 3.1 of the Kairos Document.*

6. *What new insights did you gain from the Kairos Document about the nature of Christian reconciliation? Would these insights change any of the opinions stated in your discussion of no. 4?*

If participants think that the Kairos Document overreacts to the problem being cited here, it may help to offer some further description of the South African reality. For example, it is common that white South Africans get very defensive when they begin to feel black anger directed at them. In such a situation, it is common for whites to urge a spirit of reconciliation as a means of defusing black anger. The Kairos Document authors are trying to remind us that true Christian reconciliation cannot take place without some genuine repentance that is also accompanied by efforts to redress the injustices involved.

Study Session III

Materials needed:

> Photocopies of Participant Material (p. 163 above)
> Copies of the Kairos Document, section 3.3
> Blackboard or pad of paper and writing tools

For background to this session, see above Part II, "Church Theology," especially pp. 89–94 of Sheila Briggs's essay and Josiah Young's contribution (pp. 99–101).

1. *Most North Americans form their images and their ideas about South Africa from the major print, radio, and television media. List all the images that come to mind when you hear the phrase "violence in South Africa." Now make another list of images prompted by the phrase "self-defense of South Africans." Try not to think too much about it; simply name the images that first come to mind. Save these lists for later reference.*

This study session begins by asking participants to freely associate all images that "the media" provide pertaining to two phrases: "violence in South Africa" and "self-defense of South Africans." Some participants will find this frustrating and may ask "what kind of violence?" or "which South Africans?" But the intent of the question is to see which images surface first, so it is important that people name the images that come to mind rather than the ones for which they think the questioner is looking. All participants should have something to contribute here unless they have never tuned into any media coverage of South Africa. A mixed group will likely have different associations with violence if they draw their information from diverse sources. Blacks killing other blacks as well as police brutality are a few likely responses. Other appropriate responses that are perhaps less likely to have been gleaned from the most popular media include naming some institutionalized source of violence. Examples would include malnutrition in the Bantustans or the way in which the migrant labor system splits up families. As leader you are not, however, requested to volunteer these examples since it is important that the list reflect only that to which participants have previously been exposed. Simply record those images that participants voluntarily associate with the two phrases in question.

2. *Read section 3.3 of the Kairos Document.*

3. *Share with each other any new insights gained from reading this material. What is new for you about the way in which these themes are treated by the Kairos Document?*

Allow the usual opportunity for participants to share insights gained from the reading.

4. *Return to the lists of images made in no. 1. How do you think the authors of the Kairos Document would describe the biases reflected in these lists? Which side of the struggle in South Africa would they say that the items on these lists reflect? What kind of balance does our media give us on the "violence" theme? Do we get a different kind of balance with regard to the "self-defense" theme?*

The intent of this discussion item is to help participants self-critically reflect on the bias of their primary sources for information about southern Africa. Some groups have a tendency to become defensive during this exercise. For this reason it has been suggested that the list of free associations be created on the basis of "what the media gives you" rather than "what you know." It is hoped that people will find it easier to critically evaluate the media than their own level of understanding. But you will want to help participants think about how difficult it is to transcend the biases of one's primary sources.

If your group reaches a point where it becomes aware of how limited its sources are, you can point out the special advantage Christians have over the secular society if we take advantage of the information provided for us by our sister churches in southern Africa.

Bear in mind that the discussion question asks how the Kairos Document authors would identify the bias underlying the terms we use to name "violence" and "self-defense." Many participants tend to articulate their own opinions on this issue. But the objective here is to encounter the views of South African Christians rather than to justify ourselves to ourselves.

Finally, this discussion item asks you to compare the general bias found in one list with the other list. Many groups report that their associations with the "violence" phrase reflect a mixture of what black and white South Africans would name as violence. However, the list of associations stemming from the "self-defense" phrase tends to more uniformly reflect a white South African perspective.

5. *In 1985 and again in 1986, the South African government declared a national state of emergency that imposed dramatic new levels of press censorship along with other restrictions. Discuss how such censorship is likely to bias the perspective of those North Americans who rely on the media as their primary source for information about southern Africa.*

This discussion item is designed to help groups reflect on how the South African state of emergency limits popular North American exposure to that situation. If discussion participants can agree that they face problems in this regard, it will be useful to point out that Christians could increase their reliance upon the international church as a source for some reliable information on world issues.

6. *Norwegians are proud of the way they resisted Nazi occupation of their country during World War II. Such resistance included ruthless assassination of Nazi collaborators who were called "Quislings." The French underground also threatened collaborators with deadly violence. U.S. media at that time lauded these tactics as heroic acts of self-defense. With fewer weapons at their disposal, and a larger problem of collaboration, black South Africans have evolved a resistance strategy called "necklacing." While the Western press condemns this as barbaric, black South Africans point out that this strategy has been highly effective in thwarting white* *efforts to recruit new collaborators. Is necklacing found on your list of associations with the phrase "self-defense of South Africans"? Do you think that black South Africans have more or less reason than the Norwegians and French to fight collaborators?*

Be sure that all participants hear or read this brief statement about French and Norwegian resistance to the Nazis. Perhaps some participants will have additional information to share about it. Once these circumstances have become familiar through short discussion, raise the question about whether black South Africans have more of less reason to resist collaborators. As your discussion turns to the South African comparison, check to be sure that all members of your group are familiar with necklacing as a tactic of assassinating black collaborators by fixing a burning tire around the victim's neck. Help participants to ask the sensitive question of whether necklacing was found on your group's list of associations with the self-defense phrase. If not, what can be learned from this about the biases with which we gain our exposure to southern Africa?

Before the session ends, assign homework to participants concerning research on anti-apartheid agencies (see "General Notes to the Discussion Leader," no. 4, above, pp. 158–160). A list of these agencies is provided on pp. 181–184, below. Participants should report back during Session V.

Study Session IV

Materials needed:
> Photocopies of Participant Material (p. 164 above)
> Copies of the Kairos Document, section 4.4
> Blackboard or pad of paper and writing tools

First, it is important to set a context for approaching Chapter Four of the Kairos Document. Begin by reviewing Chapter Two's critique of State Theology and Chapter Three's critique of Church Theology. Then inform your participants that today's study session will look at Chapter Four, which is called "Toward a Prophetic Theology." It may help to remind participants of the prophetic tradition in biblical history.

For background to this session, see Part IV above, "Prophetic Theology," especially pp. 120–123 of Cornel West's contribution.

1. *Recall the history of the American Revolutionary War and* *the resistance to British colonial rule. Was the violence of American patriots in that situation justified by their struggle against the British? By what factors do you reach your conclusion that such tactics were or were not justified?*

The first discussion item asks participants to recall some U.S. Revolutionary War history. While this is crucial for setting the discussion context, be sure it doesn't get lengthy. Discussion of this issue could easily take up the whole hour. Note that in addition to asking whether violence was justified in that revolution, the question asks participants how they formed their opinions.

2. *Read section 4.4 of the Kairos Document.*

3. *Discuss those points from your reading of section 4.4 that represent new perspectives for you.*

Facilitate the usual sharing of fresh insights after reading a new section of the Kairos Document.

4. *List the various types of violence required to perpetuate the apartheid system. List both direct and indirect types of violence including any violent effects that result from the continuation of that apartheid.*

Quickly make a list of all the different types of violence enacted by the State to perpetuate apartheid. Tie the discussion to section 4.4 about inevitable violence of a tyrant. Be sure to include both overt forms of violence as well as the less obvious effects of institutionalized violence such as malnutrition in the Bantustans, effects of the migrant labor system on family life, effects of an inferior educational system, etc.

Participants who are well informed about the situation in South Africa will name some aspects of violence that the media refer to as "black-on-black" violence. In many cases, the South African authorities bear direct responsibility for this type of violence. For example, during the summer of 1986, it was widely reported that black "vigilantes" in the squatters' township of Crossroads were attacking the homes of so-called comrades. After the fact, there emerged eyewitness evidence from local clergy and others who say the vigilantes receive encouragement and tactical support from police authorities.

5. *Ignore, for a moment, the long history of commitment to non-violence featured in the policies of the African National Congress (ANC) between 1912 and 1960. Today, "armed struggle" is one of many ANC strategies to end apartheid. List the various* types of violence currently employed by South Africans trying to overthrow the apartheid regime.

Discussion of this question will help participants to compare the level of violence that the apartheid system is responsible for with the violence of those who are resisting the apartheid system. A listing of the violence that resisters perpetrate can include neck-lacing, random bombing, attacks on police stations, and sabotage of public facilities. To further the comparison being developed in discussion questions nos. 4 and 5, ask participants "How long has the violence of apartheid been going on?" and compare that with the relatively recent rise of resistance violence.

Some discussion groups will include participants who have been victimized by the propaganda that white South African authorities extensively disseminate in North America. Evidence now shows that blacks under the employ of the State often disguise themselves as apartheid's resisters and then terrorize rural black populations in an effort to discredit the anti-apartheid fighters. While the outside world has often been fooled by these tactics, local populations have not. Local church leaders have helped to unmask these tactics, but it is still likely that some North Americans will report such things as "mass kidnapping of school students" as the work of apartheid's resisters. If this occurs, it may help to ask participants to identify their information sources and think criti-cally about their reliability. As leader, you must remember that it remains a problem to discuss these issues in an already propa-gandized situation. This is yet another example of how the human context in which discussions take place reflect the biases of those who participate.

6. *In his book* The Riddle of Violence, *Dr. Kenneth Kaunda, President of Zambia, recalls the period of 1965 when a renegade white minority government in Rhodesia declared itself independent from Britain. This unilateral declaration of independence was a means by which white Rhodesians tried to evade British pressure for greater black political rights. At that time, Kaunda urged the British to avert a certain outbreak of civil war by using moder-ate force to impress upon white Rhodesians the need for change. Britain, claiming to prefer a "non-violent" solution, instead opted for economic sanctions. Kaunda points out that Britain's so-called non-violent policy resulted in fifteen years of civil war that claimed 20,000 lives before blacks finally got the right to vote in what is* *now Zimbabwe. The South African government and the ANC both claim that their violent tactics are necessary to counter each other's violent posture. Keeping in mind what you have read in section 4.4 of the Kairos Document, which side is God calling you to align yourself with at this* kairos *moment?*

This is difficult discussion item. Its purpose is to help participants consider the terrible choices facing Christians in southern Africa. Make every effort to consider the issues in light of the theology presented by the Kairos Document authors.

Most North Americans prefer to believe that a choice between the violence of apartheid and the violence of its resisters can be avoided. Many of these people maintain principled opposition toward any identification with violent forces in southern Africa. But black South Africans cynically note that these same North Americans who criticize the ANC for its violent tactics are largely unaware of their own government's military relations with Pretoria. South Africans also abhor violence but are less insulated from the actual effects of violence. Enveloped by violence, South Africans feel compelled to address choices that North Americans prefer to avoid.

The struggle of this discussion is crucial to identifying with the terrible situation in which the South African churches find themselves. For those who refuse to discuss this question on the grounds that neither side should be chosen, the following paragraph may help you to understand how North Americans are already involved with violence in southern Africa. This will also aid in understanding why the Kairos Document authors are so strident in their call to take sides.

The Kaunda material provided in Study Session IV, no. 6, may help the group to consider whether a limited show of force can avert a more dramatic escalation of violence. Another avenue your discussion can take is to consider whether neutrality is possible, even if desirable. The orientation toward tyranny adopted by the Kairos Document suggests that God is calling for committed involvement in the struggle against apartheid at this crucial hour of *kairos* opportunity. Many North American Christians will argue, however, that it is possible to make a committed choice of resistance against apartheid without supporting groups such as the ANC, which pursue violence as one tactic in their resistance strategy.

Many black South Africans are cynical about the opinions of U.S. taxpayers who criticize the ANC for its violence but remain naively unaware of the direct military cooperation between the U.S. and South Africa. Immediately prior to the writing of this material, the U.S. media interpreted passage of a mild sanctions bill against South Africa as a sign that the U.S. had taken the lead in pressuring Pretoria for change. Just two weeks earlier, there was virtually no publicity given to the defeat of a bill that would have required congressional debate before continuing to fund South African sponsored "contras" seeking to overthrow the government of Angola. In 1986, the U.S. spent between 15 and 30 million dollars in a program of covert military assistance to these Angolan rebels. Critics charge that this amounts to a direct military alliance with Pretoria that is far more serious than the routine cooperation of information sharing and training programs that exist between the armed forces of the United States and South Africa. For this reason, black South Africans grow increasingly bitter when North Americans refuse to support the ANC on the basis of its armed tactics.

Study Session V

Materials needed:
> Photocopies of Participant Material (p. 165 above)
> Copies of the Conclusion of the Kairos Document

For background to this session, see above Part V, "The Kairos Covenant."

1. *Read the Conclusion of the Kairos Document.*

2. *Listen to reports from those members of your discussion group who used the homework suggestion to research available action opportunities.*

In "General Notes to the Discussion Leader," no. 4 (pp. 159–160 above), we suggest a "homework" exercise that participants can begin working on at least two weeks in advance of Study Session V. That exercise suggests that the list of anti-apartheid agencies found at the end of this discussion guide (pp. 181–184) be used by individuals who want to get better acquainted with them.

Draw the attention of your participants to this phrase at the end of the second paragraph in the Conclusion of the Kairos Document: "We call upon all those who are committed to this prophetic form of theology ... to take up the action with other related groups and organizations." Then give participants a chance to share with the larger group what they learned from their homework.

3. *What new relationship with southern Africa will you be motivated to seek as a direct result of studying the Kairos Document?*

This question offers participants a formal opportunity to commit themselves to the kind of action that the Kairos Document authors call for. You should solicit commitments that are both of personal and collective natures. In other words, encourage individuals to declare their intentions in addition to any actions that the discussion group as a whole may want to take.

4. *Has discussion of the Kairos Document had any influence on your theology? If so, what?*

A central purpose of this discussion guide is to enrich the theology of North Americans through contact with an opportunity to restate any insights into Christianity that have been occasioned by their discussion of the Kairos Document.

5. *What steps, if any, will you take to gain further exposure to the theology of "oppressed Christians"?*

The Kairos Document illustrates a vitality that can be found in the theology of many oppressed Christians. If this discussion has been a positive experience for your group, consider how you can gain access to more theology of oppressed Christians. Recall here the leader's note no. 3 for Study Session I (p. 167 above). There it was pointed out that theology will either reinforce or transform persons depending upon how representative is the community in which it is done. Bearing in mind the current demography of the global Christian family, help your group ask itself what steps can be taken to improve contact with Christians from the nations of the South.

WORSHIP SUGGESTIONS

An invaluable resource for learning the music of the churches of South Africa is now available. Fjedur is a Swedish folk choir that toured the churches of South Africa in 1978 and, in their words, "met a song more powerful than any we had ever known." As a result, Fjedur today records and teaches "songs of protest and praise" from the churches of South Africa. A collection called "Freedom Is Coming" is available both on audio cassette and in a songbook of lyrics and music for four-part harmony. Both can be ordered from Fortress Press by calling 1-800/FORTRES.

Depending upon the time available and the setting for your discussion of the Kairos Document, an opening devotion may be appropriate at each of the sessions. The following could be used or adapted for your opening session.

1. Begin with a familiar hymn stressing community in Christ.

2. Read 1 Corinthians 12:12–26.

3. Pray this prayer:

Dear God,
we give you thanks for the whole of your creation
that means so many things to us.
We are alive on this day by the means of your grace.
We thank you that you have claimed us as your own
through a baptism in Jesus Christ
that joins us to a family spread all around the world.
Thank you for this opportunity today to gather as your people
in this tiny corner of your wider creation.
Help us to turn our busy minds and many attentions
to the call of your Word for unity.
Open our group to a new movement of your Holy Spirit among us.
Lead us beyond ourselves
to encounter another community of Christians in southern Africa.
Curb our sins of racial and national pride
that we may receive from African Christians new inspiration
for how to read the Scriptures and what they call us to do.
Give us the strength not to be frightened when we sense
that our national or economic interests are being threatened.
And lead us by the example of your crucified son

— whose name we bear —
toward new life with all the people of God.
In Jesus' name we pray.
Amen.

You can create a similar plan of hymn, scripture reading, and
prayer for each of the other discussion sessions. For a conclud-
ing prayer, the following text is suggested:

O giver and taker of life,
we call upon your holy name in humble prayer.
Look with compassion upon all victims of apartheid,
in Namibia,
in South Africa,
and in other places in southern Africa
where South Africa's army has raided.
Your people there want a chance
to be as fully human as you have created them to be.
They did not ask to be put into their situation,
just as we did not of our own free will
choose to be born in the richest society in the world.
We pray urgently for a new movement of your Spirit in our midst.
Convict us with a passionate thirst for justice
that moves us to transcend our narrow, privileged perspectives
through a new commitment
to the larger community of your whole church,
for the sake of which Jesus
and some of his followers
have died.
Amen.

ANTI-APARTHEID AGENCIES

Africa News, Box 3851, Durham NC 27702; 919/286-0747. This bi-weekly, 16-page digest is the best U.S. source of current news on Africa. It covers the entire continent and provides analyses of U.S.-Africa relations. Nearly every issue has at least one story from southern Africa. *Africa News* is written in a concise, objective manner. Essential for specialists, it is also valuable to the average person who may not know much about Africa but wants to start learning. A regular, individual subscription costs US$30 a year. A prepaid trial subscription of two months is available for US$5.

American Committee on Africa (ACOA) and **The Africa Fund,** 198 Broadway, New York, NY 10038; 212/962-1210. ACOA was founded over thirty years ago to promote an end to colonialism in Africa. Today this focus continues regarding independence for Namibia and political equality for blacks and whites in South Africa. The committee provides national leadership for the "divestment movement" on U.S. campuses and in city and state legislative bodies that control public funds. The Africa Fund is ACOA's tax-exempt educational and humanitarian affiliate. The fund provides clothing and medical supplies to African refugees. It also sponsors extensive research and has published a large number of books and pamphlets on apartheid and its U.S. links. Send a self-addressed, stamped envelope for a free copy of the Fund's literature list.

American Friends Service Committee (AFSC), 1501 Cherry St., Philadelphia, PA 19102; 215/241-7169. AFSC has a "Southern Africa Program" based at its Philadelphia headquarters, which sponsors research and publication about apartheid and its U.S. connections. The committee has been active in the divestment movement and offers humanitarian and developmental assistance to many parts of Africa. It has an effective network of offices in major cities across the U.S. Several local offices employ staff members who have expertise on southern Africa and eagerly seek cooperation with other church and community groups.

Amnesty International (AI), 304 West 58th Street, New York, NY 10019; 212/582-4440. Amnesty International monitors the status of political prisoners throughout the world and reports to its supporters by means of publications. A key strategy is the formation of local chapters that "adopt" one or more specific prisoners, including many being held in South Africa and Namibia. For more information, contact AI's southern Africa coordinator, Suzanne Riveles, 9007 Garland Avenue, Silver Spring, MD 20901; 301/585-6428.

Clergy and Laity Concerned (CALC), 198 Broadway, New York, NY 10038; 212/964-6730. This interfaith network has fifty chapters throughout the U.S., which concentrate advocacy efforts in two major areas: (1) disarmament and economic justice and (2) human rights and racial justice. Membership is $20 per year and includes a subscription to *Report,* published eight times a year. Consult the New York City office to find out which chapter is nearest you, and then investigate whether the chapter has a strong southern Africa program. If not, CALC can be an excellent locus for starting such a program in your community.

Episcopal Church People for a Free Southern Africa (ECSA), 339 Lafayette Street, New York, NY 10012; 212/477-0066. ECSA is run by a well-informed advocate, William Johnston, who has cultivated close ties with the Christian community in South Africa and Namibia for the past three decades. He frequently provides his supporters with timely documentation about urgent developments in southern Africa that are sometimes not well covered anywhere else. A contribution should accompany a request for inclusion on the mailing list.

Interfaith Center on Corporate Responsibility (ICCR), Room 566, 475 Riverside Drive, New York, NY 10115; 212/870-2928. Representing broad ecumenical sponsorship, ICCR has researched the impact of U.S. corporations in South Africa for more than fifteen years. It is a clearing-house and coordinating agency for its members to challenge corporate policies and practices through shareholders' resolutions, boycotts, management consultations, or other methods designed to advocate improved corporate responsibility. For $25 per year, subscribers can receive ten issues of *The Corporate Examiner,* which reports on current corporate practices and the results of challenges by church investors.

International Defense and Aid Fund for Southern Africa (IDAF), Box 17, Cambridge, MA 02138; 617/491-8343. IDAF has a remarkable record in pursuing its three objectives: to aid, defend, and rehabilitate the victims of unjust legislation and oppressive and arbitrary procedures; to support the families and dependents of such victims; and to keep the conscience of the world alive to the issues at stake. Based in England, the fund produces excellent books, maps, and even some films. Its bimonthly publication, *IDAF News Notes,* includes a useful chronology of contemporary events in southern Africa. A subscription requires a minimum contribution of $8.

Lawyers Committee for Civil Rights Under Law—Africa Project, 1400 I Street NW, Washington, DC 20005; 202/371-1212. This organization is especially important for lawyers and others interested in the legal dimensions of apartheid. In addition to funding legal counsel for people accused of political crimes, the committee sends observers to some "security trials" and occasionally undertakes litigation to promote human rights in international law. An annual report of its work is available upon request.

National Council of Churches—Africa Office, 475 Riverside Drive, Room 612, New York, NY 10115; 212/870-2646. This ecumenical office has close contact with churches in Africa and can supply referral services as well as information about the situation in southern Africa.

Theology in a Global Context, 475 Riverside Drive, New York, NY 10115. This is a new ecumenical agency that seeks to provide North American Christians with a larger global context for doing theological reflection. Some Christian publications written outside the U.S. are available, including a regular series of helpful homiletical notes called "Preaching in a Global Context," which can be ordered at a cost of $4.50 per year.

TransAfrica, 545 Eighth Street SE, Suite 200, Washington, DC 20003; 202/547-2550. Calling itself a "black American lobby for Africa and the Caribbean," TransAfrica recently spawned the Free South Africa Movement of the U.S. by leading a year's worth of civil disobedience demonstrations in front of the South African Embassy in Washington, D.C. For several years, TransAfrica has led a cultural and sports boycott of South Africa. Today its Free South Africa Movement has grassroots contacts in dozens of U.S. cities and an aggressive anti-apartheid organizing agenda.

United Nations, United Nations, New York, NY 10017. In addition to having official international responsibility for Namibia, the United Nations represents very strong international opinion about the problem of racism in southern Africa. Two U.N. departments are especially significant for those following southern Africa issues: Office of the Commissioner for Namibia and Center Against Apartheid. Individuals can write to each of these offices separately and request to be put on the mailing list for documents published in English.

Washington Office on Africa (WOA), 100 Maryland Avenue, Washington, DC 20002; 202/546-7961. WOA is a lobby for Africa sponsored

by church and labor groups. Its primary focus is on legislation affecting
southern Africa, and its lobbying efforts depend on grassroots support
in order to be successful. WOA publishes research through a tax-exempt
educational fund. It also publishes a newsletter concerning pertinent developments on Capitol Hill. The newsletter is available for a contribution
of $10 or more per year. The WOA "Africa Hotline" — 202/546-0408 —
gives a three-minute recorded message with weekly updates about anti-
apartheid news in Washington and around the nation.

Your Church. Many denominations produce a variety of printed and
media resources about the situation in southern Africa and their work
there. Contact your church directly to investigate what may be available
for the use of your congregation.